THE ILLUSTRATED BOOK OF

# Business Strategies for
# Digital Transformation

## Learning Theory & Practice

**Alexandre Oliveira**

1

2

# Content

# List of figures

# Collaborate

In certain parts of this book you will see the following image.

Figure 1- Reader's collaboration

When you click on this image, you will be redirected to the **Reader's Form**. It is a simple way to capture your contribution and enhance the next reader's experience.

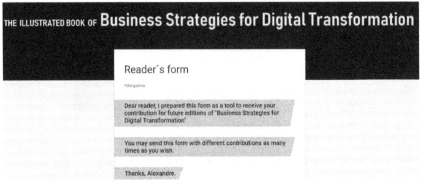

Figure 2 - Reader's Form

Whenever a new edition of this book is released, I will acknowledge the readers whose suggestions were added to the core material.

I am counting on you!

Alexandre.

# Acknowledgements

My special thanks to Professor David Rogers from Columbia University, and Geoffrey Parker, Visiting Scholar and Research Fellow, MIT Initiative on the Digital Economy (IDE). They offered a fantastic experience during Postgraduate Diploma in Digital Business (PGDDB) (EMERITUS Institute of Management, in collaboration with Columbia Business School & MIT).

I would also like to thank the multi-cultural PGDDB cohort. There were nearly 300 experienced professionals from a few dozen countries and the peer learning experience was amazing.

Finally, I would like to thank my family – Anne, Gabriel and Pedro, who followed the 12 months of this book project.

# About the author

Alexandre Oliveira is founder-partner at CEBRALOG, a supply chain consultancy and training company head-quartered in Brazil since 2001. [Brazil] [Europe] [Cebralog Linkedin]

Alexandre co-founder of the Global Society for Digital Transformation (Global Digit), a non-profit initiative focused on the impact of digital transformation.

He offers MBA courses at many business schools and is a regular contributor to seminars, conferences and congresses.

Academic background:

- Post-graduate Diploma in Digital Business (jointly offered by MIT Sloan Management (USA) and Columbia University (USA) via Emeritus Platform, 2018/19). Alexandre achieved IVY SCHOLAR prize (Top 10%) and distinction for all three building blocks: Digital Strategies for Business, Digital Transformation (platform strategies) and Digital Marketing.

- Certified Blockchain Expert (Blockchain Council, Canada, 2019)

- PhD candidate researching the impact of Artificial Intelligence on corporate governance and supply chain (2016/19) at Unicamp (Brazil), where he is guest lecturer in the extension course "Data Science for Managers and executive"

- Certified member of the board of Directors by IBGC (CCI, 2018);

- MBA in Finance (Unicamp, Brazil, 2008)

- MSc in Logistics and Supply Chain Management from Cranfield´s University School of Management, UK. Prize for the best thesis of the year (1999/2000)

- BA in Chemical Engineering (Unicamp, Brazil, 1995)

Alexandre began his career in the industry where he acquired experience in manufacturing, quality assurance and logistics in Procter & Gamble in Brazil and Europe. Over the last fifteen years, he has developed his career as a consultant, advisor and coach in companies such as 3M, Adidas, Avon, Bayer, Cargill, Eaton, GE, John Deere, Monsanto, Motorola, PepsiCo, Pernod Ricard, Sony, Syngenta, Unilever, Walmart and many others.

Since 2001 Alexandre has actively influenced logistics thinking about several supply chain organizations. He chaired the Logistics Committee at the American Chamber of Commerce (Amcham, Brazil, 2001-2004), chaired the Supply Chain Committee at the British Chamber of Commerce (Britcham, Brazil, 2006-2007) and he was Regional Vice-President of the former Brazilian Logistics Association (2002-2003). He has lectured on MBA courses since 2004 in top regional universities such as the State University of Campinas (Unicamp) and the University of São Paulo (USP).

Alexandre has published in journals such as the International Journal of Physical Distribution and Logistics Management and coordinates the Operations and Supply Chain Group at Linkedin which has nearly 35,000 members (January 2018).

Alexandre has also been President of the Brazilian Institute of Supply Chain Professionals (I.B.S.) since 2007. [I.B.S. Linkedin]

Five books published by Pearson Financial Times Press, New York, USA:

- Customer Service Supply Chain Management: Models for Achieving Customer Satisfaction, Supply Chain Performance, and Shareholder Value. 2 Editions.

- Executing the Supply Chain: Modeling Best-in-Class Processes and Performance Indicators. 4 Editions.

- Managing Supply Chain Networks: Building Competitive Advantage in Fluid and Complex Environments. 4 Editions.

- Supply Chain Management Strategy: Using SCM to Create Greater Corporate Efficiency and Profits. 2 Editions.

- A Guide to Supply Chain Management: The Evolution of SCM Models, Strategies, and Practices. Kindle Edition.

Co-author of the book Crisis Management: A Leadership Perspective, (2015, Nova Science Publishers, NY-USA). Responsible for the chapter on global humanitarian operations supply chain governance.

# Introduction

As in any strategic initiative, digital transformation practices must be treated as movements that happen across the entire organization – it is not the responsibility of any specific department nor an area of knowledge.

Associating efforts and benefits of digital transformation to the area of information technology is a simplistic approach. The digital ecosystem of a company must be thought of, built and maintained from the collegiate work of multiple areas, including IT, marketing, finance, sales, operations and supply chain management.

**Different faces of digital transformation.**

There are many words and expressions that have appeared in the recent dictionary of Digital Transformation: digitization, disintermediation, intermediation, disrupture, innovation, asymmetric competition, frenemies, coopetitors.

--------------------------------

Suggested reading

**Digital Ecosystem**

Digital ecosystem: how can your business benefit from one? by M. Bennett

What Is a Digital Ecosystem? by Andrew Zangre

**Asymetric competition:**

Who competes with whom? by DeSarbo, Wayne, R. Grewal, and J. Wind

**Frenemies:**

Partner or Competitor? Frenemies in Business by H.O. Maycotte

**Coopetition:**

What is Coopetition? by Sara Toole

--------------------------------

There are also many technologies and practices associated with digital transformations: descriptive, predictive and prescriptive analytics, artificial intelligence (and machine learning and deep learning), data mining and process mining, robotic process automation (RPA), robotics, internet of things (IoT), big data, blockchain, virtual reality (VR), augmented reality (AR), etc. These terms will be dealt with at some point over the 12 case studies chosen to comprise this book.

We will, for now, explore a line of reasoning that I used while lecturing on digital transformation. Summarizing everything into one sentence:

> *"The digital transformation that really adds value is the transformation of a company's business model, which becomes a way of delivering a unique value proposition to potential consumers on an unprecedented scale and having technology as a mere facilitator."*

Therefore, we will not focus on technological transformation in this book – although we enjoy the accumulated result of decades of technological evolution. Instead, we will talk about strategically rethinking business models, repositioning in the market and reshaping the relationships with competitors and partners.

Digital transformation is not driven by innovation or creativity – although these elements are part of the construction of business models capable of delivering value to the consumer. Digital transformation deals with decisions in the corporate governance environment in order to ensure organizational endurance.

**Digitization**

In some situations, digital transformation may occur without changing the business model. In this case, the value proposition may be associated with a more comfortable experience or increased productivity – and consequent reduction of operating costs.

For example, there are several companies that make the intermediation of loads between industries and carriers. This intermediation has always existed in the offline world.

Although the exchange of information happens in a faster and complete way, the added value to the parties remains the same. Truckers get a load. Industries can get truckers.

Although there are advantages over the offline model, digitalization is limited because it does not truly transform the business model and does not deliver a truly new value proposition. However, it is one of the faces of digital transformation.

--------------------

Suggested reading
Digital Freight Matching Services & Technologies by Jeff Berman
--------------------

Figure 3 - Freight Matching Services

Some companies that are part of the Freight Matching Services ecosystem in the USA are: Uber, Amazon, Kuebix, Fourkites, Cargomatic, Convoy, CargoX, Transfix, uShip Pro, Convoy, Load Express, Next Trucking, C.H. Robinson, Hub Group, XPO Logistics, Coyote Logistics, and Total Quality Logistics.

14

## Disintermediation

Digital transformation can produce another effect called disintermediation. In this case, there is a significant change in the business model, usually substituting two or more links of the traditional value chain by a new native digital player.

The disintermediation agent usually comes up with a new value proposition and connects the source of the resources to the final consumers. The classic example is Netflix.

However, it occurs in different industries (please read "The gatekeepers must go: How disintermediation is changing business models", by Nick Hoffman). The opportunities for more distributed manufacturing and supply-chain disintermediation are becoming even more appealing with 3D printing, for example.

----------------

Suggested reading

40 3D printing experts give predictions for additive manufacturing in 2019

----------------

The process of disintermediation is marked by long conflicts between incoming players and incumbents. The outcome can occur in several ways, as we will see in the cases throughout this ebook.

## Intermediation

Another typical process of digital transformation is intermediation. Facebook acts as an intermediary agent between the traditional media companies – such as newspapers and news agencies – and final consumers (readers).

The most common value proposition in intermediation is associated with the convenience of a recommendation mechanism when the intermediary agent is able to uniquely understand the behavior and needs of consumers – thus, they can offer services or products with a high degree of customization.

15

Figure 4 - Auto Tech Startups

Source: Joseph Michael

The startup ecosystem represents a new form of intermediation. For example, in the automotive industry startups have proliferated and now offer a large number of new solutions – they are intermediating connectivity between people, machines and devices.

----------------------

Suggested reading

- The 12 Automotive Startups to Watch in 2019
- Start-Ups Are Disrupting The Automotive Industry by Sarwant Singh
- Disintermediation and intermediation beyond theory by Peter B. Nichol
- The digital platform strategy of new publishers" by Grzegorz Piechota.
- Mastering the intermediaries by B. Edelman

----------------------

The example of this replicability barrier is Uber. Do you know some of Uber's competitors? See these: Lyft, Curb, Didi, Grab and Ola, just to name a few.

The fact that Uber achieved great economies of scale before the others was due to gaining access to digital consumer behavior data. These data are used as strategic assets (thanks to different technologies) – we are inimitable.

**The more of these assets, in the form of consumer behavior data, the better the business model, the greater the ability to customize solutions and the lower the possibility of being achieved by the competition.**

A virtuous cycle is formed. In this book we will also discuss the design, launch and governance of digital platforms that allow this type of business model.

-----------------------------------------------------------------------------------

**The Rise of Platform Businesses** / Platforms represent a fundamental shift in how businesses relate to each other—from linear to more networked business models. Platform businesses can often be very light in assets but generate large revenues. Instead of building features and seeking to get customers to use their own products, they build ecosystems by encouraging customers to interact with each other.

- Retail: Taobao, eBay, Amazon Marketplace [what is a marketplace platform?]
- Media: YouTube, Forbes.com
- Advertising: Google, Baidu, Craigslist
- Finance: PayPal, Kickstarter, Alipay
- Gaming: Xbox, PlayStation
- Mobile computing: iOS, Android, Xiaomi
- Business software: SAP, Oracle, Salesforce
- Home appliances: Philips, Nest
- Hospitality: Airbnb, TripAdvisor
- Transportation: Uber, Didi
- Education: Coursera, Udemy, Khan Academy
- Recruiting and job search: LinkedIn, Glassdoor
- Freelance work: Upwork, Amazon Mechanical Turk
- Philanthropy: Kiva, DonorsChoose

-----------------------------------------------------------------------------------

From Rogers, 2016, pp. 54–55

The current business model can be affected (challenged) by a process of digital transformation via intermediation or disintermediation; There is a serious dispute between the players of the traditional model and the proposed model. The incumbents may use several strategies to react to the threat – we will discuss these strategies in the case studies of this book.

Disruptive situations do not occur when a new business does not challenge an existing business model. In this case, the entrants do not challenge incumbents, but take advantage of niches associated with unmet consumers´ needs. In this case, even if the offer of an unmatched value proposition occurs, there is no traditional business model to be replaced – Therefore, disruption cannot occur.

The way incumbents react to the menace of digital transformation is a key topic in this book. To become familiar with this subject, read the article "When worlds collide: why your company's digital transformation effort is stalled" (by George Corbin, Harvard Business Review Digital Initiative).

### Innovation

*"- And what is innovation? - What is new."* It is both a superficial and comprehensive concept. The word innovation does not imply the generation of value. (*see Merriam-Webster definition*) We can innovate, change and get worse. Digitization, intermediation, disintermediation and disrupture are examples of innovation.

### The role of technology

The different cases presented in this document will refer to technologies – and technology applications. However, despite the fact they are needed tools, they are not the starting point for digital transformation thinking.

It is up to the company to follow a trail with a path of steps:

1. Understand its current business model;
2. Understand the unmet needs of its customers;

3. Understand the value proposition that should offer its customers to position themselves differently in the market;

4. Involve several areas of the organization and develop a business model capable of delivering the value proposition to the customers;

5. Understand how technologies can be used as enablers of the business model described in Item 4;

------------------------------------------

Suggested reading

- Digital transformation is not a technology issue By Dorothée Laire

- Digital Transformation Is About Change by P. Weill & S. Woerner

- Digital Transformation - It's Not All About Technology by Kunal Patel

- Digital transformation is about people, not technology by Martha Heller

------------------------------------------

**Understanding the potential digital customers**

What's the difference between these businesses? Taxis & Uber; Marriott & Airbnb; Avis & Zipcar? The latter, which are known as disruptive companies, were able to design business models that have gone beyond their established customers and reached the entire market of potential consumers.

---------------

Suggested reading
From Avis to Zipcar by Kathryn Gessner

---------------

The Apps (*what is an APP?*) they use are interfaces (not the business model) capable of approximating the digital native companies of many people in a short period of time. What brought the new companies closer to the consumers was not the "App", but the innovative value proposition that is offered through a business model that challenged a traditional structure.

We discuss once again the business model transformation and value proposition capable of meeting the unmet needs of potential consumers. This is the real benefit of a well-made digital transformation. Or, if a company is the traditional player threatened, the role of the digital transformation reacts appropriately. This paper will deal with both situations.

**The organizational structure**

The proper design of the organizational structure is fundamental to the success of a journey of digital transformation.

The Digital Transformation Steering Committee must consist of internal members (company employees) and external members, grouped into two levels: the leadership team and the engagement team.

Figure 5 - DT Steering Committee

The leadership team is a smaller group, led by the Digital Transformation Officer. The internal members also have the Information Technology (IT) business partners and a small multifunctional group of leaders from key areas to meet the goals of the digital transformation journey.

As external members, it is recommended to have someone native to the digital age (early adopter mind), a specialist in digital transformation (independent

20

digital strategy expert) and a professional who can represent the most traditional thoughts, typical of incumbent companies.

The engagement team is larger. It involves the whole leadership of the Organization (C-suit, board-members, CEO) and the average leadership (middle management). Representatives from key customers or strategic suppliers may join this group. Despite not leading the digital transformation, these people are opinion makers. This team should be cared for and prepared as a vital strategy for organizational success.

Having introduced the topic, let us discuss the case studies.

# Case McDonald's

## 1. McDonald's & DY: more than meet the eyes

McDonald's has recently acquired of the Israeli company Dynamic Yield, specialized in Artificial intelligence, for US $300 million. The largest acquisition in the last 20 years is apparently aligned with a service that is not relevant to shareholders.

We need to look at the corporate governance environment – especially at the board of directors, its composition and its decisions. To facilitate the reading, I arranged the content in 20 questions and answers (responded in February, 2019).

----------------------

Suggested reading

- McDonald's is acquiring Dynamic Yield to create a more customized drive-thru by Anthony Ha
- McDonald's Bites on Big Data With $300 Million Acquisition by Brian Barrett
- What McDonald's acquisition of Dynamic Yield tells us about digital transformation by Larry Dignan

------------------------

**1. McDonald's has recently announced the acquisition of the Israeli company Dynamic Yield, specialized in Artificial intelligence applications for the end user. Did this US $300 million move surprise you?**

This acquisition is another stage of a strategy that began in 2015, consisting of three pillars: retaining current customers; recovery of recently lost customers: and attracting new customers. Three priorities were chosen: "Digital", "Delivery" and " Experience of the Future". The acquisition of Dynamic Yield is aligned with these priorities. More at Growth Strategy.

## 2. What are the objectives of these three priorities?

- "Digital" looks at consumers' journey within the Eat-in, Shopping for travel (Take Away), Drive Thru and Order Delivery services.

- "Delivery" emphasizes the "order delivery" service as this market is now dominated by various local digital native companies such as iFoods, UberEats and Rappi that act as intermediaries between the restaurants and consumers.

- "Experience of the Future" focuses on the use of technology within restaurants (emphasis on Eat-in). The goal is to attract consumers from breakfast to late-night snacks and encourage the increase in the average ticket value.

----------------------

Suggested reading

- iFood is testing market deliveries in São Paulo
- Uber Eats launches its new platform for corporate accounts
- Rappi raises $200M as LA tech investment reaches new highs

-------------------------


## 3. Is it possible to say that the corporate strategy emphasizes the experience within restaurants and delivery services, while Drive Thru and Take Away activities are relatively less Important ones?

Yes. The consumption in restaurants represents a greater share of the demand. the effort to increase the number of consumers and the average ticket spent makes sense.

Concerning delivery, what is at stake is the dispute for the digital consumer, many of them are not yet used to going to the McDonald's restaurant – it is an opportunity to increase the customer base.

On the other hand, Take Away and Drive Thru reach a smaller slice of the current organic demand. They do not have the same potential to increase the consumer base as the "order delivery" does, nor does it have the relevant revenue share from the Eat-in model. However, the increase in the average tickets of these two services can generate significant gains.

**4. In which of these four strategies did the acquisition of Dynamic Yield focus on?**

It focused on the Drive Thru experience. The announcement made on March 25 (2019) indicates that the chain will use technology to vary menu views on Drive Thru panels based on the time of day, weather and traffic, as well as to instantly suggest additional items for customers´ requests based on current selections. The company will also integrate technology into self-order kiosks.

**Link to video:**
https://youtu.be/wsBtRjiB4-o

**Link to the announcement:**
McDonald´s & Dynamic Yield

**5. So, does this acquisition not address the key strategies (Eat-in and Delivery)?**

Nothing was mentioned in the official statement of March 25th.

However, a letter dated 11 April 2019, addressed to the shareholders, S. Easterbrook (President and CEO) cites that "Delivery" is already available in more than half of the restaurants and that it represents US\$ 3 billion/year (although they have "only scratched the consumer's understanding of this service").

In the same letter, he says that they have already converted half of their stores into the "Experience of the Future" model, increasing revenue in the Eat-in format with more visits and greater spending per customer.

He does not cite the services of Drive Thru and Take-away in this letter to the shareholders.

**6. Is it not strange that the largest acquisition in the last 20 years is apparently aligned with the Drive Thru, a service that is not relevant in the president's letter to shareholders?**

The President's letter speaks of "providing delicious moments for families and customers and for generations to come." As I cited, there have been ongoing actions since 2015 that suggest that the acquisition of Dynamic Yield has goals far beyond those announced at this time.

**7. What actions are these? Are these secret movements?**

They're not secret. But it requires a watchful eye for a part of the organization that tends to be distant from the perception of the general public. We need to look at the corporate governance environment – especially at the board of directors, its composition and its decisions.

**8. What does the McDonald´s corporate governance environment tell us?**

Currently there are 12 members on the board of directors, 11 of them independent (including the Chairman). According to the preparatory document for the next shareholders' meeting, which will take place in Dallas on May 23, 2019, 5 of the directors have been members of the board since 2015.

Moreover, they arrived with a new profile. The average age of the new members is 58 years old, and the youngest is also the CEO Easterbrook, who is 51 years old. The other board members are aged 66 years on average.

While older members have strong expertise in finance, the most recent ones have work experience in retail and consumer goods companies – some have expertise with digital consumers. These companies include Google, Nike, Target, Groupon, Compass (foodservice) and Fedex.

### 9. But the CEO Easterbrook is an insider ….

Yes, right. But, even though the young CEO sits on the board, the Chairman of the Board of Directors is an independent member. E. Hernandez (Chairman) is also the CEO of InterCom Security Systems, a global company with 35,000 employees, familiar with technological applications - including in the sector of Services and consumer goods.

### 10. What is the impact of the current composition of the McDonald´s board?

They are members with experience as CEOs in companies and sectors of the economy where the behavior of the new digital consumer offers more impacts. This is essential for the company to overcome cultural inertia and reposition itself for the next few decades. The acquisition of DY is proof of this cultural victory.

### 11. But if this board is more on the ball, what drove McDonald´s to acquire Dynamic Yield based on improving the Drive Thru experience if, as you said, the most important is the Eat-in and Delivery experience?

First, because Drive Thru is not unimportant. But not all decisions are declared at once. I am sure that this acquisition goes far beyond the Drive Thru experience and that it considers all the risks of the business environment today and over the next several years. As I said, the CEO himself said that today's actions also look at "the generations to come."

## 12. And what are the main risks in the business environment at McDonalds?

Many of these risks are detailed in the annual report that the CEO sends to the Securities and Exchange Commission (SEC) - the main American regulator of the stock market. In the last report, signed in February 2019, some risks drew attention because they can be mitigated by the developments from the application of technologies that Dynamic Yield has.

## 13. What are these risks?

There is the risk of reducing the number of customers in restaurants due to competition with the home delivery service, reducing operational profitability - especially if there is dependence on intermediaries such as iFooDs, UberEats and Rappi.

There is also the change of behavior concerning the consumer and their eating and leisure time habits. The customer's journey is perceived only from when he/she goes into the store until he/she pays for the product.

The growing complexity of the menu and options of purchase and delivery puts in check the balance between service level and operating costs. Restaurant capacity management requires decisions from new parameters every day. Delivery, which is growing, competes for the attention of the restaurants' resources.

There are risks associated with the lack of visibility of consumer experiences. Eat-In, Take-Away, Drive Thru and Delivery experiences of the same consumer are not integrated.

There is also the risk associated with the maintenance and performance of the equipment required for operating each restaurant. In a business that has increased its portfolio, equipment wear increases and the risk of breakage (and breakdown of revenue) also increases. The ability to predict the behavior and failures of the equipment becomes more relevant.

### 14. Do you see other risks?

McDonalds is highly intensive and expensive in terms of marketing and promotional campaigns. These are mass strategies that reach the entire population with standardized messages. There is a risk of not sensitizing their specific target audience to the extent that the portfolio increases and targeting strategies are not sophisticated.

The consumer behavior of "informal Eating out" changes quickly and the competition is dynamic. The current pricing strategy is fairly slow and outdated. The ability to offer dynamic prices based on point conditions in a region or even in a restaurant, and the possibility of offering personalized packages with unique prices, is already an expectation of the digital consumer that the McDonald´s restaurant chain is not able to satisfy.

The influence of social media should also be considered. How to monitor and react quickly and specifically when there is a negative impact on the brand?

How to monitor the thousands of processes that promote these risks and transform them into performance indicators capable of signaling in real time the sense of navigation of the company as a whole and every restaurant?

**15. Is the current McDonald ´s board of directors addressing all these risks?**

The composition of a board has "players" with different abilities. Not everyone has the profile to identify the risks associated with the digital transformation that results from the new behavior of the end user.

The next shareholders' meeting will vote for retaining 11 the current members, of which 7 have experience in marketing/digital and two in technology and cyber security.

The profile includes names such as Margaret Georgiadis (former president of Google Americas and ex-COO of Groupon). The Strategy committee will consist of four members and three of them will assume their duties from the renewal of the board initiated in 2015.

Thus, we can say that the composition of the current board of directors is prepared to identify, understand and position themselves considering the risks to the business I listed.


**16. Do you believe that the acquisition of Dynamic Yield undergoes the analysis of all these risks on the part of the McDonald ´s board of directors?**

Yes, I believe that. The positioning of Dynamic Yield offers conditions to address actions that will mitigate or limit several of these risks. Something far beyond any Drive Thru solution announced and able to contribute to the long-term success of operations and consequent continuity in the business.

### 17. But what does Dynamic Yield do?

DY is an Israeli company that uses Artificial intelligence for various applications associated with the end user interfaces – whether in omnichannel transaction environments, social media or digital touchpoints in physical stores.

Its applications include managing customer data (capturing, creating complex segmentation rules, identifying and customizing anonymous users, targeting cross-site audiences, comparing online hearings, and analyzing in real time); Omnichannel Personalization and experimentation via digital platforms (scaling content personalization, setting event-driven messages in Apps & email, deploying adaptive Recommendations); Algorithms for content and product recommendation decision making); Personalization and targeted notifications at any point in the customer lifecycle; Triggering personalized messages in applications and emails, etc...

### 18. But what is the differential of DY? There are several other companies that dominate Artificial intelligence applications....

Mastering some techniques and applications of AI is not a differential. In the case of DY we must, however, consider its customer base in sectors as diverse as ecommerce, fashion and apparel, sports, Beauty & personal care, food and beverage, consumer electronics, luxury, B2B, technology, games, travel and hospitality, among others.

There are more than 300 customers on every continent – access to consumer habits across the globe is a tremendous differential. The accumulated knowledge when deploying solutions for these companies accelerates the return on the acquisition investment. The learning of DY comes from deployments on clients such as Lacoste, Sephora, Ikea, Kendo, Forever 21 and Planet Sports.

These conditions give the members of the board of directors (and the shareholders) the confidence that the new business will be able to contribute to any customizations necessary for the chain of restaurants.

## 19. How far can McDonald's get with the know-how from Dynamic Yield?

A decision already made is to keep DY as an independent business, guaranteeing the provision of services to current customers and achieving new ones. In the announcement, it became clear that DY will meet the needs of the McDonald's (as a client) with "the commitment to expand its capacities around constantly changing consumer trends". CEO Easterbrook said new technologies will use data and implement the vision of creating more personalized experiences for customers.

Having captured the data and treated it in a sophisticated manner, McDonald's will be able to offer more value-added delivery solutions than current interme-diaries and regain lost profitability. The ecosystem built from millions of con-sumers will enable the creation of a marketplace that can sell food and conven-ience products, including competitors. It will be possible to compose orders with own and third-party products, expanding the consumer base and raising the av-erage ticket for each transaction.

Online and real-time consumer relationships associated with recommendation systems (such as Netflix) will allow consumers to suggest stops for "impulse consumption" every time a customer is in the vicinity of a store – always with menu suggestions and dynamic pricing strategies. This strategy can be applied to restaurants of other chains through specific monetization practices. Always generating data that will be able to know the new habits of consumers in order to adapt the menus.

Data captured on machine sensors in restaurants will allow the reduction of maintenance costs associated with the predictability of failures. With this there will be reduced operating costs and a consequent increase in profitability. Ma-chine learning algorithms will take care of production sequencing, whose com-plexity is increasingly pushed by the diversification of the portfolio, keeping the average attendance time.

True Omnichannel integration is possible, with ordering and delivery options on multiple channels that are combinable around effective service levels.

There will be a large reduction in the average cost of advertising (promotional campaigns, publicity and marketing) as the know-how of DY will allow the personalization of promotions at very low costs. This is aligned with an announcement made at the end of 2017 by Global vice president of Media and CRM, Bob Rupczynski, who said "money in marketing" would have to work more. In 2017, the annual budget for mass marketing revolves around US$2 billion.

Also, with the know-how of DY, McDonald´s can perform "sentiment analysis" and monitor social media and react in real time to any interaction produced in the world, strengthening brand equity.

**20. It seems that the acquisition of Dynamic Yield is just a seed that is being planted...**

In fact, the seed began to be planted in 2015 with the beginning of the process of renewing the company's board of directors. Several strategic decisions have been made since then, always in order to contribute to building knowledge about the risks associated with the digital transformation.

The acquisition of DY is another step. Like every digital transformation journey in a traditional company, the learning curve is slow. But the process has seemed to be constant in the last five years and, I believe, will be quicker in the next five.

DY was bought due to the combination of embedded expertise and the match with the current and future risks. But the operational and cultural independence of DY, promised by McDonald´s, will be crucial in allowing its natural speed of learning and adaptation so necessary to the plans of the restaurant chain. The success of this acquisition can be better evaluated in a few years.

# FMCG Case Study

## 2. FMCG: Reaching the Digital Customer

**Introducing the case**

This case presents a customer network strategy as an enabler to transform a product-based company into a digital platform business

----------------------

Suggested reading

* The Network Is Your Customer by Ivana Taylor
* The Value Of Customer Networks by Christopher Koch
* 5 Strategies to Thrive in a Digital Age by David Rogers

-------------------------

For the last twenty years, I have been working as a management consultant for clients in various industries, many of them with business based on sales channels that are dependent on large retail chains. While the retail chains build up relationships with their customers (end users or consumers), the manufacturers (retail suppliers) have no direct contact with their product users. This scenario inhibits many brand strengthening efforts.

These industries become even more vulnerable when the business environment is populated with competitors that fight for price differentiation. Some of the key characteristics of this industry sector are:
* Low-cost product manufacturer;
* Large retail stores as single (or main) sales channel;
* Increasing dependency on digital (online) marketplaces;
* Many competitors;
* No comparative advantage;
* No relationship with their product consumers or users.

The motivation to work on this industry case study came from an article published in The Harvard Business Review (HBR): Three Elements of a Successful Platform Strategy (by Mark Bonchek and Sangeet Paul Choudary). While discussing some features related to the management of multisided platforms, the authors said:

> *"For example, imagine a smart mousetrap with sensors that wirelessly communicate to a cloud-based MouseCatcher service. Homeowners and exterminators could monitor the status of the trap on their smartphones, receiving a text message when it is out of bait or needs checking. Smart traps already exist. But the shift from products to platforms would focus on building the service (the Trap Store?) that enables anyone with a smart trap to connect and communicate."*

------------------

Suggested reading

Strategic Decisions for Multisided Platforms by Andrei Hagiu

------------------

## The mouse trap company

To illustrate this case, I selected a simple product: a mouse trap. This pack with two "Victor M035 Easy Set Mouse Trap" can be found at Walmart for US$ 5.04 (Nov, 2018) with free shipping from Samis Shop.

Figure 6 - The traditional mouse trap

Samis Shop is an "everyday store" that uses Walmart marketplace. Therefore, it is likely Victor (The Mouse Trap Company since 1898) sells its products to Samis Shop, which is part of Walmart marketplace with another 70 million products. Therefore, the value chain can be illustrated as:

Figure 7 - Victor's value chain

The Mouse Trap Company has diversified its activities and now it offers products to control or eliminate several pests, including house mice, Norway rats, moles, deer mice, roof rats, gophers, wood rats (pack rats), voles and shrews.

Victor's website (in 2018) sells 145 products from 8 suppliers divided into 34 categories. There is a Learning Center where the public have access to sections such as "article and tips", "how to", "site bibliography" and the "rodent library". This company also offered the "Smart-Kill™ Wi-Fi Electronic Mouse Trap" for US$ 39.99 each (Nov 2018). This product sends kill alerts on customers' mobile devices, therefore they only check traps when alerted.

Figure 8 - Electronic mouse trap

With "Smart-Kill", customers can monitor traps from anywhere via the user-friendly mobile app that is able to control an unlimited number of traps simultaneously. If the "problem" is slightly bigger, the "Smart-Kill™ Wi-Fi Electronic **Rat** Trap" is available for US$ 59.99.

Figure 9 - Electronic rat trap

**The digital platform canvas**

I created a Digital Platform Canvas Model ® based on the article published in the Harvard Business Review by Marshall W. Van Alstyne, Geoffrey G. Parker and Sangeet Paul Choudary entitled "Pipelines, Platforms, and the New Rules of Strategy"

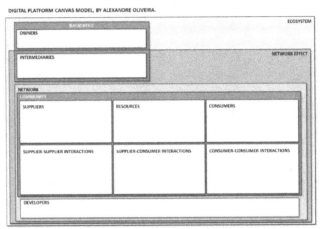

Figure 10 - Digital Platform Canvas

The elements of the digital platform are:

- THE COMMUNITY, formed by suppliers and their resources, consumers and the interaction between them;

- THE NETWORK, formed by the community and by internal and external developers of solutions that enhance the quality of network interactions;

- THE BACK-OFFICE, formed by the owners of the entire ecosystem and by eventual intermediaries that enable interactions between suppliers and consumers;

- THE NETWORK EFFECTS, which are all interactions produced between suppliers, consumers, developers and intermediaries – the goal of a digital platform is to provide high quality network effects;

- THE ECOSYSTEM, which is the group of elements in a platform.

## The existing digital ecosystem

This case study focuses on the opportunities specifically related to the mouse and rat traps. The digital ecosystem described for these products provides a limited customer experience as the potential customer strategies are not properly explored.

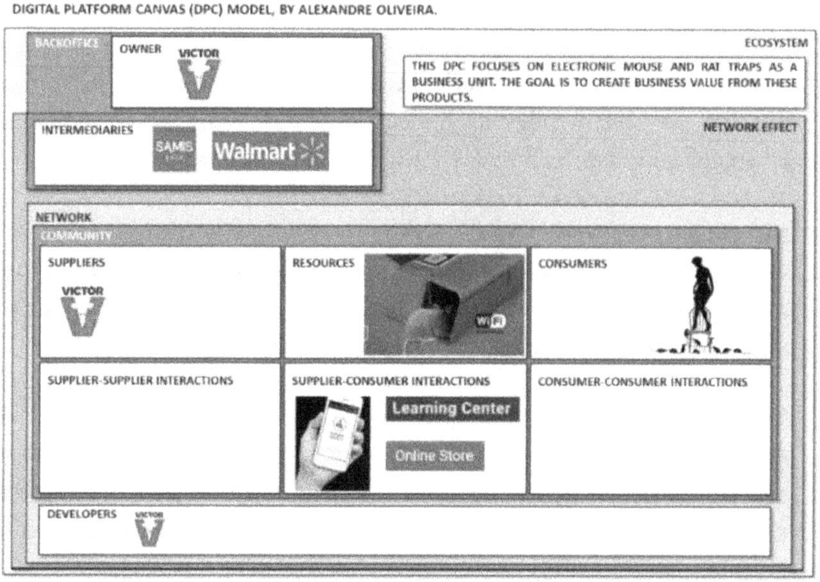

DIGITAL PLATFORM CANVAS (DPC) MODEL, BY ALEXANDRE OLIVEIRA.

Figure 11 - Victor's Digital Platform (a)

The manufacturing company (Victor) is the supplier of the traps (resources) that are bought by the consumers (householders). On Victor's website (existing digital platform), there are four types of interactions that occur through the Learning Center, the Customer Support, the Online Store and the App that informs the householder when the rodent is caught.

There are least two intermediaries (Samis and Walmart) but I am sure there are many more. Therefore, it is fair to believe a significant share of Victor's revenue is generated from the retail channel, while direct sales (usually more profitable) produce a marginal contribution to the business.

37

**Digital customer network behavior**

According to Prof. David Rogers, there are five customer network behaviors.

Access: "customer networks always seek to access their digital data and interactions more easily, more flexibly, more ubiquitously. So, anything that makes what I'm seeking on my information one step closer or easier or simpler is always very attractive."

Engage: "customer networks seek to engage with content, content that is relevant to our lives, whether it's business content for an issue we're facing, entertaining content, humorous content, lots of different kinds of content.".

Customize: "customer networks seek to customize our experiences. So, we aren't all looking for the same content, we're not looking for a one size fit all product or meteor experience in the digital world. We've been trained in the digital era to expect an incredible range of choice."

Connect: "customer networks desire to connect with others. We are social animals. This has been the driving force behind the messaging apps, the social media of all kinds as we seek to reach out to others we know and express where we are, what we're thinking, what we're seeing, and share that with other people."

Collaborate: "customer networks want to collaborate with others, to work together with others towards some kind of a shared goal, some sense of a shared project or outcome which they are contributing to with others through the various open platforms and media of the digital world."

\-\-\-\-\-\-\-\-\-\-\-\-\-\-\-\-\-\-\-\-\-\-

Suggested reading
"The digital transformation Playbook" by Prof. David L. Rogers
\-\-\-\-\-\-\-\-\-\-\-\-\-\-\-\-\-\-\-\-\-\-

## Digital interactions

The existing digital interactions with customers can be classified according to the five customer network strategies in the following figure:

| Customer strategy | | Practice |
|---|---|---|
| Access | be faster, easier, more on-demand | Online store & electronic traps with App |
| Engage | be a source of valued content | Learning center |
| Customize | be adaptable to different customer needs | - |
| Connect | be a valuable part of customers' online and social conversations | - |
| Collabo-rate | invite customers to help build your business and your enterprise | - |

Figure 12 - Existing challenges

## The digital transformation strategy: customer objectives

The strategy was planned to address the following questions:

- What can be done when traditional manufacturers of low-cost products become more vulnerable due to the growth of digital marketplaces?
- How should we react to a digital ecosystem that is weakening its relative strength within the value chain players?
- Is it possible to use data as a strategic asset and create unique brand equity?
- What can a manufacturer do to see all potential customers, when nowadays it is not even possible to see their current consumers who purchase their products?
- Will digital transformation create a long and wealthy future for low-cost product manufacturers or will it enable unique competitive advantage?

The electronic mouse and rat traps were selected because of the existing (though embryonic) digital strategy to connect with customers through an App. Now we need to define a few key customer objectives to be achieved from the digital transformation strategy:

39

1. To understand the number of potential customers by connecting to a large consumer basis; it is important to distinguish three concepts:

   - Customers: those who buy/have bought a Victor's electronic trap;

   - Consumer basis: all customers, actual and potential, who buy/have bought / will buy a trap from any supplier, including all Victor competitors and intermediaries (such as marketplaces);

   - Potential customers: part of the consumer basis which is not Victor's customers but has the potential to become a customer;

2. Create a digital ecosystem capable of attracting a large consumer basis and give them quality experience until they have a real need for Victor's products; that's when they will move from potential consumer to customer.

3. To increase cash generation based on:

   - Gaining band visibility, therefore, strengthening loyalty, and increasing retail channel sales (including online sales in marketplaces);

   - Increasing revenue generation by attracting more customers to its loyalty circle;

   - Developing direct sales channel to enhance more profitable revenue streams;

**The target customer**

----------------

Suggested reading
Target market vs Target Consumer by Lynda Moultry Belcher

----------------

In the first moment, the target customer is not yet clearly identified. In fact, the visibility of the existing potential demand and its features is one of the key expected benefits to be achieved with the new App.

While the App becomes more popular, it is expected that Victor will identify where the potential customers are located; today Victor only sees the demand signal generated by their direct sales and receives consolidated sales information from the intermediaries (such as marketplaces).

The connections and collaborations that the new App enables will outline the geographical limits of potential demand, the type of rodents that exist in these areas, the type of home where they are found (house, flat, restaurants, tourist attractions, city center, suburb), if there are seasonal aspects of the demand that is region-specific, etc.

Therefore, in the early stages of the digital transformation journey, it is possible that the target customer type has not yet been identified. In such a case, the first goal of the strategy is to provide unique insights about the consumers so that the business can be properly segmented according to precise value elements.

**The digital customer strategy**

A new and comprehensive customer strategy can be developed and implemented. The vision for the following 12 months is to transform this company from product-based business to a digital platform.

The existing APP is offered as a service exclusively to consumers that buy the electronic traps. Now, let´s assume Victor hired a small company to develop an APP aiming at promoting connection, engagement and collaboration with the customers. This new APP is available to anyone who wants information about the presence of rodents, even those who are not a Victor´s customer (see Figure 8, red arrows).

The App developer integrated the geo-positioning data to visualization features and created heat graphs to illustrate the presence of rodents in different parts of the city and the country.

This collaborative APP captures consumers' data and makes it available to the firm (see Figure 8, blue arrow). These heat graphs are available to anyone with the App and there are versions for IOS, Android and PC.

--------------

Suggested reading

- Seven data visualization techniques for location by Ryan Baumann
- Top 19 geovisualization tools, APIs and libraries by Aleks Buczkowski
- 80 Data Visualization Examples by Peter Murray
- Introducing Geo Heatmap Feature by Evan Tan

--------------

If the user wishes to contribute and update the rodent presence database, it requires a simple user-validation process, which amplifies the number of potential consumers for Victor products (see Figure 08, purple dotted lines).

The registered user may inform the App of some basic features such as body size, color, tail size, location type (garden, roof, kitchen), etc. This info is partially available to the public and strengthens the relationship with communities dispersed in various geographical regions.

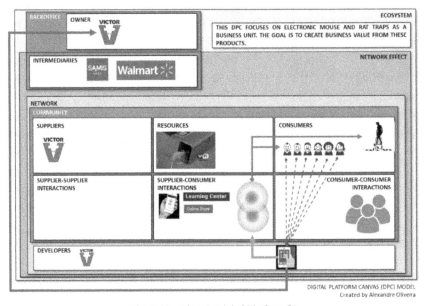

Figure 13 - Victor's Digital Platform (b)

Customized information on how to deal with specific types of animals is available to each App user based on searching criteria associated to specific rodent features.

This initiative allows the manufacturer to communicate directly with the potential consumer basis, not only actual customers. This enables a new market positioning and creates a path to reduce revenue dependency from retail channels as direct sales shall increase.

In the long term, Victor will have detailed visibility of consumer market behavior and trends which shall benefit the business in diverse ways. It will improve sales forecast and identify initial stages of growing demand areas, which facilitates prover inventory allocation and trade marketing initiatives.

Additionally, Victor may also enhance the allocation of sales force, with dynamic distribution of people according to updated information.

This is only the first step towards the devising of a massive digital platform model which can create multiple revenue streams based on customer strategies.

Although partnerships and strategic alliances are not explored in this business case, they may enhance this customer experience by bringing to the digital platform ecosystem third parties such as exterminators' business, other manufacturers of complementary products and even the public sector.

**The impact on the customer network behavior**

The idea is to implement one simple and scalable initiative that affects all five dimensions of customer strategy in a format that it accepts future enhancement.

| Customer strategy | Today | Recommendation |
| --- | --- | --- |
| Access | Online store & Electronic traps | Online Store & Electronic traps with App + NEW APP |
| Engage | Learning center | Learning Center + NEW APP |
| Customize | - | NEW APP |
| Connect | - | NEW APP |

| Collaborate | - | NEW APP |

Figure 14 - Impact on the customer network behavior

The new App increases customer access as it makes interactions "faster, easier and more on-demand" the interactions with a far wider basis of potential customers. Customers will engage with Victor as they will be able to inform the location of rodents (and time and date), which allows the platform to estimate the risk of contamination in different regions.

---------------------

Suggested reading

- Complete guide to Association Rules by Anisha Garg
- Machine Learning and Data Mining by Pier Luca Lanzi
- Association Rule Mining and its Applications by Abhinav Rai
- How do recommendation engines work?
- Types of M. Learning Algorithms You Should Know by David Fumo
- Big Data: How It's Used to Make Business Decisions by Fred Donovan
- Let's talk about Advanced Analytics
- Strategies to create value from big data by S. Parise, B. Iyer, D. Vesset

--------------------

As Victor has access to potential demand data, they can precisely allocate the quantity of traps in different regions of the city. The customization goes further as the App associates the customers profile, the data they uploaded and send recommendations on how to deal with the animals. These recommendations are generated by machine learning algorithms based on unsupervised association rules that become more precise as the database increases.

The solution created to capture data from any person and to share data processed with advanced analytics techniques enables the community to connect and collaborate to generate a complete understanding of the rodent´s presence. Every potential consumer may feel part of this community, both contributing and benefiting from its growth.

44

## Measuring the digital scenario

The performance indicators must reflect different perspectives of the business and measure if the company is succeeding to achieve the expected goals.

| Business Perspective | Performance indicator | Description |
|---|---|---|
| Market size | 1) Size of the consumer basis | Monitor the digital ecosystem participants, summing the number of registered members (those who may update info) and standard users as the consumer basis. Monitor this number on a weekly basis. |
| | 2) number of Potential Consumers | This is the segment of the consumer basis that are in selected regions considered priority market according to Victor´s strategy. Monitor the growth of potential consumers on a weekly basis. |
| | 3) number of Customers | Number of different customers who have bought a Victor´s electronic trap. Monitor this number monthly. |
| Finance | 4) $ Revenue – direct sales | Revenue generated from online sales at Victor´s ecommerce platform. |
| | 5) $ Revenue – indirect sales | Revenue that is not generated from online sales at Victor´s e-commerce platform. |
| Digital Strategy | 6) App – Registered members | A sub-group of Victor´s consumer basis. This is the number of people that actually got involved in the digital platform and contributes with information for the ecosystem. Monitor this number on a weekly basis. |
| | 7) App - number of updates | This is the quantity of interactions produced by the registered members. Monitor this indicator weekly. |
| Finance & Digital Strategy | 8) number and $ of transactions | The number of transactions and the associated revenue generated from the users of the APP. Monitor these numbers on a weekly basis. |
| | 9) Revenue from App uses vs Total Revenue | This indicator shows the percentage of revenue generated from App users compared to total Victor´s revenue. As this number increases, the dependency on indirect sales reduces. Monitor this number monthly. |
| | 10) quantity and $ from registered members | A subset of indicator (8), focused on registered members of the digital platform. |

Figure 15 - Measuring the scenario

# Healthcare Case Study

## 3. Healthcare: Dealing with Marketplaces

### Health Care Value Train

The Competitive Value Train is a visual tool presented by Prof. David Rogers in his book. Some examples include:

**Competition:** The Competitive Value Train

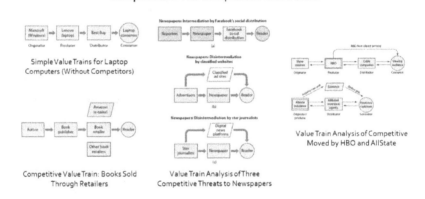

Rogers, David L. 2016 The Digital Transformation Playbook: Rethink Your Business for the Digital Age (Columbia Business School Publishing) (p. 80-82) Columbia University Press. Kindle Edition.

Figure 16 - Competitive value train - examples

In the healthcare value train, I considered the research and development (R&D) function as the core activity performed in the ORIGINATOR train and four types of players were identified: the academia and its researchers, the pharmaceutical manufacturers which maintains R&D departments, the government that is frequently involved in research in areas that do not appeal to the private sector, and the private institutions that do focused research for specific diseases such as The Bill and Melinda Gates Foundation.

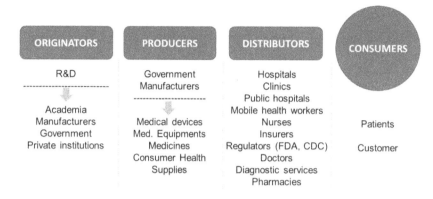

Figure 17 – Healthcare value train

In the PRODUCER train, the options are the pharmaceutical companies and their factories, eventually outsourced, and the manufacturing facilities maintained by the public sector. These companies produce medicine, equipment, devices and chemicals such as reagents that supply consumers' hospitals, clinics and diagnostic service providers.

It is in the third train, the DISTRIBUTOR's, where I found the largest variety of stakeholders. Several organizations populate this train and create multiple options to address the CONSUMER train. Here in the DISTRIBUTOR train I identified the following players: regulators (FDA, CDC), private and public hospitals, clinics, pharmacies, doctors, nurses, pharmacists, insurers, diagnostic services and mobile health workers.

Finally, in the CONSUMER train I identified two types of players: the patient and the customer. While the patients are those "receiving or registered to receive medical treatment", the customer is the person who will consume a product, not necessarily a medicine. For example, a consumer will buy a sun protection cream in a pharmacy, which does not make him/her a patient.

Following the Value Train analysis, I decided to explore the relationship between the customers and the products available in the pharmacies. This choice was made because of two main reasons.

1. Due to the market growth potential.

Sales in pharmacy's channels have raised around the globe. For example, in my country, Brazil, despite the severe economic crisis we faced from 2016 to 2018, pharmacies represent a US$ 20 billion market and its revenue increased 9% in 2017 vs 2016 (9.34% increase for medicines and 7% for non-prescribed products). (Nov,18)

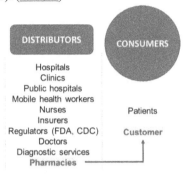

Figure 18 – Target customer

2. Due to the market coverage potential.

There are over 74,000 pharmacies in Brazil   and 94% of the population usually buy products in pharmacies regularly. Consumers are 55% women and 45% men. Over 40% of the consumers shop frequently (the average is 2 times per month).  The consumers buy medicines (88%), personal care products (42%), cosmetics (38%). And only 16% of these Brazilians see the pharmacies as a healthcare commerce – for them, they are minimarkets (31%), cosmetic shops (28%) and convenience stores (25%). (Jul,18)

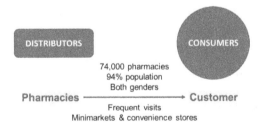

Figure 19 – Potential market

Based on this scenario I decided to explore the relationship between pharmacies and customers from the perspective of the convenience experience.

Brainstorming process – partial

| 1 MAP STAKEHOLDERS | 2 VALUE TRAIN ANALYSIS | 3 FOCUS ON PHARMA-CUSTOMERS RELATIONSHIP | 4 FOCUS ON THE CONVENIENCE EXPERIENCE |

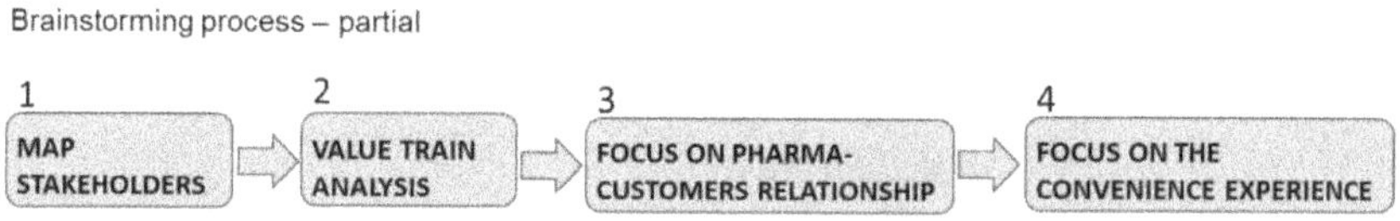

Figure 20 – Brainstorming sequence

## Market research

Using the concept of rapid experimentation, I opted to send a Whatsapp message to some of my contacts. The total number of people addressed was 128 and 36 replied (28%).

> The message sent was: *"Hello everyone! I need a little help from you. I am working on a project and I need to identify items one can buy in pharmacies that may cause embarrassment to the consumer. Please focus on products that do not require a medical prescription. I will give you some examples: men buying Viagra; women buying condoms or morning-after pills. What other products can you think of? Thanks!"*

---------------

The Seven Principles of Experimentation:
Learn Early
Be Fast and Iterate
Fall in Love with the Problem
Not the Solution
Get Credible Feedback
Measure What Matters Now
Test Your Assumptions
Fail Smart.

----------------

Rogers, 2016, pp. 134–142

The list of items suggested by the respondents is summarized in Figure 16. But the interesting thing is that several respondents suggested the embarrassment is not only product-dependent, but also context-dependent. For example, a woman may feel embarrassed by a geriatric diaper if it is for her own personal use but may feel perfectly comfortable if she is buying it for her father or mother.

**Products sold in pharmacies that may embarrass the consumer**

| MEN | WOMEN | MEN / WOMEN |
|---|---|---|
| Erectile dysfunction such as Viagra Hair coloring kits | Condoms Morning-after pill Pregnancy test | Hair loss products Suppositories Personal lubricants Laxatives Hemorrhoid creams Geriatric diapers Rehab treatments |

Figure 21 – Consumers' responses

A quick search on the web will lengthen list. For example, Buzzfeed.com lists "21 Slightly Embarrassing Products You'll Be Glad You Can Buy Online" and includes shoe spray, cat tongue brush, lice kit, gas relief medication, wart remover, bed bug spray, callus remover, dandruff shampoo or anti-diarrhea medication.

The next step in the brainstorming process is to collect information on this type of consumer behavior, which makes them embarrassed, to give me quality insights for the construction of a solid innovative idea.

**Consumer behavior**

During my search for information on how consumers buy embarrassing products, I identified three articles that provided me with several insights. These articles are from the Wharton University, Mississippi State University and the University of Manitoba:

- Embarrassing Products in the Age of Social Media with J. Berger and J. Wind

- How to Sell Embarrassing Products by C. Barney, C. Jones and A. Farmer

- Embarrassment in Consumer Purchase by D. W. Dahl, R. Manchanda and J. Argo

I listed excerpts of these articles with information that contributed to my brain-storming process. The insights consider the context of the type of consumer I have selected to focus on: those who need to buy embarrassing products for personal consumption.

| Excerpts from the articles | Insights |
|---|---|
| "If the typical purchaser …. believes he or she can mitigate embarrassment by filling up the shopping cart with cough drops, tissues or other distraction items, …." | - Consumers spend more than they need to. |
| "Even mild embarrassment can cause consumers to alter their behavior in an effort to avoid the sting of unflattering evaluations," the study notes. | - Consumers are very sensitive. |
| "… Consumers found endcaps — the displays on the end of an aisle — more embarrassing, which caused anxiety, and were likely to avoid them in favor of an in-aisle location". | - Pharmacies acknowledge the problem and have tried to address the issue. |
| "Privacy bags or baskets may also help shoppers feel more anonymous as they walk around the store with their selection." | |
| "… the use of vending machines (as condoms are often sold in public bathrooms). Using vending machines to sell embarrassing products may be a way in which stores can successfully minimize embarrassment, as customers can make their purchase without having to interact with employees." | - But in-store solutions are not easy. |
| "Some customers would rather risk breaking the law and stealing certain products than being embarrassed by purchasing them. Some retailers have reacted to this by locking up embarrassing products, | - Consumers tend to go online. |

| | |
|---|---|
| thus requiring employee interaction to get the product. Understandably, this can depress sales — no one wants to ask a clerk where to get the hemorrhoid cream." | - Online sale is an option |
| "This is particularly pertinent given the decline of in-store sales for these items. Consumers are moving toward purchasing their embarrassing — and non-embarrassing — products online ..." "It's much easier, and less embarrassing, to order online. Online has also made it easier to collect information and commiserate with other people that have the same issues — all anonymously, which reduces embarrassment." | - But on-line experience may also be uncomfortable |
| "You are creating a history now, and people know your privacy is non-existent, so there is a data list of what you've ordered," says Kahn. "Some people are deathly afraid of it." | - Consumers may feel guilty of buying these products, even when no one else is seeing them. |
| "... when individuals are alone, they can experience various types of affective responses (e.g., guilt, excitement) resulting from imagining others." | |

Figure 22 - Consumer behavior

## The unmet customer need and the business offer

From Culture & Digital Transformation: How a 145-Year-Old Insurance Company Became A Digital Darling; HB (Hilton Barbour) and MS (Michael Shostak)

*"HB: We began by talking about Sonnet as an example of Digital Transformation in Insurance but your story seems more about Culture as the Transformation.*

*MS: It's actually both. Sonnet is a digital transformation for sure but there's nothing particularly unique about how we've tackled that from a technology perspective. When folks ask me "How were YOU able to do this ahead of some of the larger, more expected players in the category?" I go back to a simple Venn diagram I always use. If you can: 1) intersect an unmet customer need—and the unmet part is critical; 2) with a changing business model and; 3) an enabling technology, you're golden.*

*Do it with 2 out of those 3, you're likely to be successful for a while at least."*

It is now possible to clearly state the unmet customer need – therefore, to produce a relevant business offer. The unmet customer need is the possibility to have an anonymous shopping experience for embarrassing healthcare products (commonly only available in pharmacies), with expert advice, at a fair price, without feeling guilty.

Figure 23 – Brainstorming process

## The business offer

- The business offer is a digital platform model that will use stakeholders' interactions to enhance four out of five digital customer behaviors (access, engage, connect and collaborate).

- The business model will use data from the product, service and customer as a strategic asset to build a unique experience, different from what is currently available on the market.

- The business offer will address four value templates (insight, targeting, personalization and context) to produce unique value proposition generatives with exclusive value network components that will create barriers to avoid competitors' imitation. (Jan,19)

Therefore, the challenge is to create a digital platform model that offers an outstanding anonymous shopping experience, for embarrassing healthcare products, for buyer's own consumption (commonly only available in pharmacies), with expert advice, at a fair price, without feeling guilty.

| Insights: Revealing the Invisible: | Targeting: Narrowing the Field |
|---|---|
| Customer psychology (How are my brands or products perceived in the marketplace? What motivates and influences customer decisions? Can I predict and measure customer word of mouth?).<br><br>Customer behavior (How are buying habits shifting? How are customers using my product? Where is fraud or abuse taking place?).<br><br>Impact of specific actions on customers' psychology and behavior (What is the result of my change in messaging, marketing spending, product mix, or distribution channels?). | Today, advanced segmentation schemes can be based on much more diverse customer data and can produce dozens or even hundreds of micro-categories.<br><br>How a customer is targeted can change in real time as well, as they are assigned to one segment or another based on behavioral data such as which e-mails, they clicked on, rewards they redeemed, or content they shared.<br><br>Ideally, customer lifetime value should be included as one metric for targeting customers based on their long-term value to the business. |
| **Personalization: Tailoring to Fit** | **Context: Providing a Reference Frame** |
| Once businesses are targeting micro-segments of customers, the next opportunity is to treat them each differently, in ways that are most relevant and valuable to them. | How one customer's actions or outcomes stack up against those of a broader population<br><br>Putting data in context is at the heart of the "quantified self" movement—evidenced by customers' rising interest in measuring their diet, exercise, heart rates, sleep patterns, and other biological markers. |

Figure 24 – Data templates [16]

## The incumbents

Although the products that our type of consumers buy are usually available in pharmacies, this is not the only way to acquire them. Each sales channel offers specific value proposition and represents a category of incumbent.

To create a solid disruptive strategy, my business offer must consider each six categories of incumbents (pharmacies, retail stores, online stores, marketplace, focused online stores and expert Apps), otherwise it may disrupt one incumbent but will fail to build barriers to inhibit other incumbents to imitate.

A summary with the key features for each category of incumbent is presented in the following Figure. I offer a brief description for the category, its strong value element (from the perspective of the target consumer) and the negative characteristics associated.

| Incumbents | 1 Pharmacies | 2 Retail Store | 3 Online Store |
|---|---|---|---|
| Type of experience | Physical | Physical | Online |
| Brief description | Traditional sales channel | Alternative to traditional sales channel | Traditional business' online stores |
| Value elements | Better price<br>Variety<br>Expert advice | Better price<br>Variety of camouflage | Large variety<br>Anonymous |
| Negative characteristics | Not anonymous<br>Feeling guilty<br>Extra expenses from camouflage items | Not anonymous<br>Limited variety<br>No expert advice<br>Feeling guilty<br>Extra expenses from camouflage items | No expert advice<br>Feeling guilty<br>Digital footprint<br>Personal contact at delivery<br>Product visibility to neighbors |

| Incumbents | 4 Marketplace | 5 Focused online store | 6 Comparative sites |
|---|---|---|---|
| Type of experience | Online | Online | Online |
| Brief description | Multi product stores, not associated to a specific retail brand | Online stores focused on items that may cause embarrassment | Convenience solution for online purchase in pharmacies |
| Value elements | Large variety<br>Better price<br>Longer delivery time<br>Anonymous | Large variety<br>Anonymous<br>Q&A for recurrent questions | Large variety<br>Price comparison<br>Anonymous |
| Negative characteristics | No expert advice<br>Feeling guilty<br>Digital footprint<br>Product visibility to neighbors<br>Personal contact at delivery | No live expert advice<br>Feeling guilty<br>Digital footprint<br>Personal contact at delivery | No expert advice<br>Feeling guilty<br>Digital footprint<br>Product visibility to neighbors<br>Personal contact at delivery |

Figure 25 - Detailing the incumbents

In pharmacies, the consumer will find the best prices, a wider range of target products and expert advice from pharmacists. However, there are disadvantages:

- The purchasing experience is not anonymous
- The consumer tends to spend money on unneeded items to camouflage the target products and
- The feeling of being alone (the only one buying that product) produces the guilty sentiment.

Purchasing in large retail stores tends to enhance the camouflage experience. It also offers a competitive price, but the variety of the target products is limited when compared to the pharmacies. In these stores the consumer will not find expert advice, and the purchase is not anonymous as it is likely that a neighbor is also around. The large variety of non-target products may serve as camouflage at a lower cost when compared to a pharmacy.

Buying the target products from pharmacy online stores guarantees access to a large variety of target products but it tends to be more expensive because of the delivery rates.

However, there are some negative points:

- The digital experience does not offer the opportunity to meet a pharmacist and receive quality technical advice.
- The consumers' concern about the digital footprint is increasing.
- There is no guarantee the product will not be visible to the neighbors at the moment of delivery.
- The customers will not be comfortable as they may be giving up both a fair price and an expert´s advice

The difference may be a slightly better price enabled by the higher distributed volumes. But this positive effect may be balanced by a longer delivery lead time when compared to local pharmacy online purchase.

Online purchases in marketplaces will offer an experience similar to what the consumer finds as described in one of the articles cited (Embarrassment in Consumer Purchase: The Roles of Social Presence and Purchase Familiarity), some sites, such as shopinprivate.com offer products that give new purpose to the word unmentionables, while prominently trumpeting policies regarding "privacy, security and discretion" in their sales pitch.

The company's mascot, Mister Private, pledges to "defend you in the face of nosy neighbors, chatty mailmen and leering customers at your local drugstore". This focused online store represents a very strong incumbent. But the overall experience is associated to doing something weird, awkward or wrong – therefore the guilty feeling remains. And the delivery boy in front of your door will know you are buying something which is to be hidden.

Finally, the sixth group of incumbents is formed by sites (or Apps) that compare prices of healthcare products in different places. One example is Pharmacychecker.com which offers an experience similar to a generalist market place, but with a wider range of target products and the possibility of finding better prices. However, the negative characteristics are the same.

| Master incumbent | |
|---|---|
| Value elements | Negative characteristics |
| Better price (pharmacies)<br>Large Variety (market places and comparative sites)<br>Live expert advice (pharmacies)<br>Anonymous (online experiences)<br>Short delivery time (pharmacies' online stores)<br>No digital fingerprint (pharmacies or retail)<br>Price comparison (comparison sites) | Minimum physical contact (online channels - contact with the delivery guy)<br>Feeling guilty (all options)<br>Neighbors may have some visibility (at least in the moment of product delivery or while you are in the store). |

Figure 26 - The master incumbent

To design a bold strategy, invulnerable to any of these categories, it is required to aggregate each category in one distinct group – as one very strong incumbent. I call this the Master Incumbent. Therefore, a disruptive solution should be able to simultaneously deliver all value elements listed for our imaginary Master Incumbent and disrupt the three remaining negative characteristics.

## The target customer

The target customer is the consumer with the following unmet need: an anonymous shopping experience for embarrassing healthcare products (commonly only available in pharmacies), with expert advice, at a fair price, without feeling guilty.

## The new value propositions

The challenger business is based on a digital platform model. The platform has four suppliers: a marketplace, a community of pharmacists, a community of doctors and the platform owner. Each supplier is responsible for delivering one or more resources to the platform. The community of pharmacists will provide expert advice for the consumers. The platform owner will develop the ecosystem which is made available to consumers through a mobile App and a desktop version.

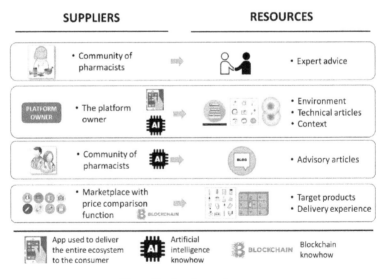

Figure 27 – Suppliers and resources

The platform uses artificial intelligence (AI) algorithms based on machine learning to search for technical articles related to any product trades in its market place – the AI knowhow is available to consumers via a user-friendly interface, so the consumer can guide all the necessary searches. Other machine learning algorithms will capture product, process and consumer data and provide a context to each consumer– this is explored in the following sections of the case.

The community of doctors will contribute to short articles via personal blogs integrated to the ecosystem. The artificial intelligence knowhow will automatically read key works in each text produced and link them to target-products and to the technical articles cited before.

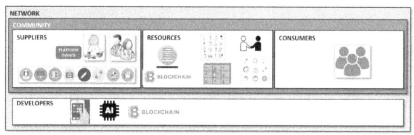

Figure 28 – The community and developers

Finally, the marketplace will offer price comparison solutions including on-line and off-line stores. The blockchain technology will ensure unique data security and disable the possibility of creating a digital footprint. The marketplace is also responsible for creating the best-possible target-product delivery experience to the consumer.

-------------------

Suggested reading

What Is Blockchain Technology? A Beginner's Guide by Chantelle Lafaille

-------------------

## Delivering the value elements

How to deliver better value than any incumbent type (Figure 29) and as strong as the value delivered by the hypothetical Master Incumbent, which combines the value elements of each incumbent's type.

| Master incumbent value elements | How the digital platform is delivering this value |
|---|---|
| 1. Better price (pharmacies) | The marketplace with price comparison tools guarantees a large variety of items and the possibility of finding very competitive prices. |
| 2. Large Variety (market places and comparative sites) | Additionally, the App has a tool that allows consumers to insert product prices in different pharmacies. This will strengthen the COLLABORATION behavior as the consumers will contribute to the entire platform. Therefore, even if someone is a geriatric diaper user, he or she may upload the pricing data of a completely different product such as lime shampoos. |
| 3. Price comparison (comparison sites) | |
| **Master incumbent value elements** | **How the digital platform is delivering this value** |
| 4. Live expert advice (pharmacies) | The community of pharmacists will contribute by answering the consumers' questions. The more answers the pharmacist responds and the higher the satisfaction of the consumer with the answer, the higher the classification of the pharmacist in the platform ranking. The platform ranking gives visibility of the pharmacists for future interactions with consumers on the platform. |
| | The community of pharmacists will have a limited number of professionals, to be defined as a proportion of the consumers' community size. Each pharmacist is a strategic stakeholder of the platform and will receive a share of the revenue generated in the marketplace. The higher the position in the rank, the higher the payment will be. |
| | A very clear code of ethics will ensure no pharmacist is regularly recommending specific products and brands, nor recommending unnecessary medication and not recommending high-end price products. There are clear communication channels so that any consumer that feels uncomfortable with the pharmacist's behavior has the chance to make anonymous complaints. |
| | The quality of the community of pharmacists is a key point to strengthening the digital consumer's behavior ENGAGE. The credibility of these people and the trust in their information is a strategic asset for the platform. |

| 5. Anonymous (online experience) | The entire experience on the digital platform is online. |
|---|---|
| | The blockchain technology applied to each purchasing event will ensure unique data security and disable the possibility of creating a digital footprint. |
| 6. No digital fingerprint (pharmacies or retail) | There is no sign-in procedure using social media, therefore it is not possible for Instagram, Facebook, Linkedin, etc. to track any of your online activities. |
| 7. Short delivery time (pharmacies' online stores) | The comparison tool used by the marketplace has filtering options according to the geo positioning of the product sellers (i.e. Pharmacies, retail stores) and compares its delivery lead times to the delivery lead-times of other online stores. |
| | This cognitive system is executed with machine learning algorithms (artificial intelligence techniques). |

Figure 29 - Master incumbent – the value elements

## Disrupting the negative characteristics

How to disrupt the negative characteristics present in all the incumbent types.

| Master incumbent negative characteristics | How the digital platform is delivering this value |
|---|---|
| 1. Minimum physical contact (online channels - contact with the delivery guy) | For those consumers who are so sensitive that even quick contact with the deliverer at his/her door causes embarrassment, or the possibility that a neighbor may have access to any information related to the target product purchased, there is the possibility of picking up the product in lockers located in areas with limited public traffic. There is no human contact. |
| 2. Neighbors may have some visibility (at least in the moment of product delivery or while you are in the store). | The consumer types a code number generated when the transaction is confirmed, and the locker opens automatically. This service has an extra charge. |
| | This operation is widely known as click and collect. Some variations include the option to collect the product in-store without extra charges. The possibility to offer multiple purchasing and fulfillment combination enhances the overall omnichannel consumer experience. |
| 3. Feeling guilty (all options) | This is the most difficult negative point to overcome. |
| | Properly addressing this issue will represent a clear solution differentiation. |
| | This item is detailed in the following section (what is in your value network?). |

Figure 30 - Master incumbent – negative characteristics

## Value proposition - summary

|  |  | Brief description | Value elements |
|---|---|---|---|
| Incum-bents | 1 - Pharmacies | Traditional sales channel | Better price<br>Variety<br>Expert advice |
|  | 2 - Retail Store | Alternative to tradi-tional sales channel | Better price<br>Variety of camouflage |
|  | 3 - Online Store | Traditional business online stores | Large variety<br>Anonymous |
|  | 4 - Market-place | Multi product stores, not associated to a specific retail brand | Large variety<br>Better price<br>Longer delivery time<br>Anonymous |
|  | 5 - Focused online store | Online stores focused on items that may cause embarrassment | Large variety<br>Anonymous<br>Q&A for recurrent questions |
|  | 6 - Compara-tive sites | Convenience solution for online purchase in pharmacies | Large variety<br>Price comparison<br>Anonymous |
| New business offer | Digital Plat-form Model | A digital ecosystem where the communi-ties of customers and other stakeholders can freely interact and generate value to each other | Better price<br>Large variety<br>Expert advice<br>No need for camouflage items<br>Anonymous<br>Price comparison<br>Technical information<br>No digital footprint<br>It is possible not to have any hu-man contact<br>Sense of belongingness (guilty feeling disrupted) |

Figure 31 - Value proposition - summary

## The value networks

Think of the different components – the people, assets, partners that are going to allow this new startup business to deliver the new offering to the market. What different pieces will you need to put together in order to get this startup off the ground?

- The value network lies in four types of interactions, as illustrated in the following image:

62

- consumer-consumer interactions;
- consumer-pharmacist interactions;
- consumer-doctor interactions; and
- consumer-market place interactions.

The existence of these interactions depends on the ability of the digital platform model to deliver value to consumers, pharmacists and doctors. If any of these stakeholders do not value the experience on the platform, they will leave it and the business model will be ruined.

The existence of these interactions depends on the ability of the digital platform model to deliver value to consumers, pharmacists and doctors. If any of these stakeholders do not value the experience in the platform, they will leave it and the business model will be ruined.

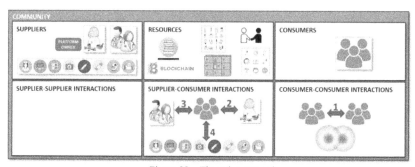

Figure 32 – The value network

## Value network in the consumer-consumer interactions

This type of interactions, illustrated at the bottom right of Figure 28, is meant to enhance digital customers´ behaviors: CONNECT and COLLABORATE. As a consequence, an important value template is: CONTEXT. Finally, it is by positioning the consumer within a context that the platform model will disrupt the third negative characteristic of the Master Incumbent: feeling guilty.

The dynamics expected for these interactions is preceded by the construction of a solid community of pharmacists, a relevant community of doctors and the technological backbone providing information based on artificial intelligence tools. In other words, to ensure fast and easy ACCESS (a digital customer behavior) to the platform, the platform's suppliers should be organized and actionable.

The COLLABORATE behavior occurs when the customer contributes to improving the platform. It occurs when the customer updates pricing information of a target-product, when they evaluate the performance of the pharmacists, when they evaluate the quality of an article or when they classify the relevance of a doctor's text in the blogs. This collaboration produces PRODUCT, SERVICE and CONSUMER data that is captured by the platform owner as a strategic asset.

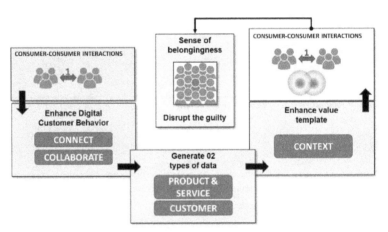

Figure 33 – Value network in the C2C interactions

The second behavior is CONNECT. The platform allows the consumer to interact and create topic-related communication channels. The trends related to the channels created and the intensity of communication within consumers in each channel is valuable data for the platform owner. Again, there is an intense generation of strategic data.

The machine learning algorithms will process the data produced and captured during consumer-consumer interaction and generate several statistics that include the number of users in the platform that have a certain embarrassing health problem or that buy some specific embarrassing target product.

These data analytics are shared with the entire platform community, so each consumer will perceive they are not alone in this situation.

The consumer will realize that there are many people sharing the same needs – and some of them may be geographically very close. The combination of this awareness and the possibility to connect enhances the feeling of belonginess which disrupts the feeling of guilty.

The more these consumer-consumer interactions occurs, the more visibility the platform owner will have on the consumer behavior. By investing in this strategy that reveals the invisible, the platform strengthens the value template of INSIGHT which may promote future TARGETING and PERSONALIZATION strategies. This data generation and data management environment is unique, different from the type of data available to the existing incumbents and impossible to be imitated.

**Value network in the consumer-pharmacist interactions**

---------------

Suggested reading
Why consumers trust pharmacists

-----------------

As explained, "the quality of the pharmacists' community is a key point to strengthen the digital consumer behavior ENGAGE. The credibility of these people and the trust in their information is a strategic asset for the platform".

The possibility of evaluating the pharmacist's interaction enhances the COLLABORATION behavior and generates product, service and customer data for the platform. These interactions can also provide relevant data for TARGETING and PERSONALIZATION as machine learning tools can compare text and voice data produce and associate this to specific target-products available in the market place.

## Value network in the consumer-doctor interactions

[*Do you know doctor.com?*]

These interactions are not as direct as pharmacist-consumers. Based on the analysis of the consumers' behavior, it is recommended that they read specific short articles written by doctors and will have the chance to evaluate the content according to how clear and useful it is.

Doctors whose articles are evaluated better will be top ranked in the categories the articles are focused on. Being top ranked means their names will be on the top of the list in case consumers want to arrange an appointment for a consultation.

Therefore, this may become a source for revenue generation for the doctors as well. These interactions strengthen the ENGAGE consumers´ behavior, associated to the technical credibility of the digital platform they are interacting in.

## Value network in consumer-marketplace interactions

This is the fourth type of interaction. From the consumer perspective, the marketplace offers variety, price comparison and several delivery options – including pickup in a locker, which is completely anonymous. From the platform's perspective, this is the interaction that supports the monetization strategy. Despite the fact this is the main revenue stream, it must be managed as a consequence of the high-quality experience in the first three types of interactions.

--------------------

Suggested reading

**Digital Platforms Monetization**

- Options to monetize thei audience by L. Markidan
- Metrics to support 'your' digital monetization strategy by Adam Singer
- We all have digital assets, why not monetize them?

--------------------

## Value network - summary

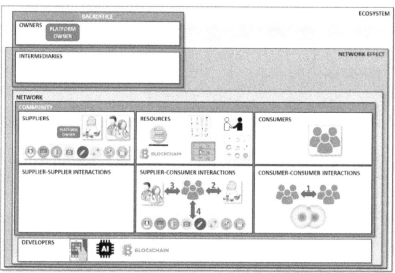

Figure 34 – Value network – summary

## Barriers to imitation

Which of these is different from the incumbent? Can the incumbent match them? Is the value network capable of offering a barrier to imitation?

67

The platform ecosystem is based on high value network effects generated by unique stakeholders' interactions that produce data managed as a strategic asset.

This virtuous cycle retains the existing customers and attracts more new customers to the platform. Once the business offer has accumulated massive information about customer behavior, the capacity to design precise TARGETING and PERSONALIZATION initiatives will ENGAGE customers so strongly that they will advocate for the platform.

The asset that cannot be imitated is the data captured from consumer behavior during the interactions within the platform model

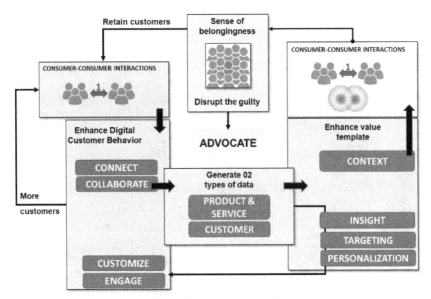

Figure 35 – Barriers to imitation

**Displacing the value of the incumbents**

It would have to dramatically displace the value of the incumbent – be much better, at least in the eyes of some of its customers. This business offer is the only one to simultaneously deliver the value elements of each incumbent.

Additionally, it is the only one to deliver three specific value elements: no digital footprint, possibility to follow the Path-To-Purchase with no human contact and – more importantly – it is the only model that disrupts the guilty feeling and creates a sense of belongingness within the consumers.

|  |  | Value elements |
|---|---|---|
| Incumbents | 1 - Pharmacies | Better price; Variety; Expert advice |
|  | 2 - Retail Store | Better price; Variety of camouflage |
|  | 3 - Online Store | Large variety; Anonymous |
|  | 4 - Marketplace | Large variety; Better price; Longer delivery time; Anonymous |
|  | 5 - Focused online store | Large variety; Anonymous; Q&A for recurrent questions |
|  | 6 - Comparative sites | Large variety; Price comparison; Anonymous |
| New business offer | Digital Platform Model | Better price; Large variety; Expert advice; No need for camouflage items; Anonymous; Price comparison; Technical information; No digital footprint; It is possible not to have any human contact; Sense of belongingness (guilty feeling disrupted) |

Figure 36 - Value elements

# Hospitality Case Study

## 4. Airbnb vs. Wyndham

*From: How the Hotel Industry Views Its Future (and Airbnb)*

*"Joe Pinsker: You mentioned Airbnb. Is there a consensus on how hotel companies feel about it, and rental platforms like it?*

*Jeff Weinstein: I'm not sure, and some of the executives in the industry aren't sure, if Airbnb is really hurting the industry too much, because the industry has been performing so well. But at the same time, they recognize an alternative is emerging. Not only is there Airbnb, but in the luxury space, there's a site called One Fine Stay and another called Oasis, and people who have second and third houses can rent them out without having to undertake the effort themselves. So that has the industry trying to figure out, "Okay, how do we offer the same type of local experience that one would have in a home?" And that goes back to the local experiences I was describing earlier."*

In this introduction, I narrow the context of the tourism industry down to the hospitality industry, then to the lodging segment, and then through the hotel categories and guest types. According to Hayes, the tourism industry is the third retail industry following automotive and food.

It is the largest service industry in most countries and one of the largest employers. The tourism industry is formed by four industries: hospitality, retail (shopping) stores, transportation services and destination (activity) sites.

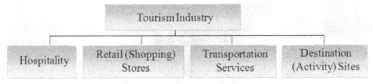

Figure 37 – The tourism industry

The hospitality industry has four main sectors:

1. lodging segment (hotels, inns, motels, pensions, resorts, bed & break-fasts, villas and cottages, guest houses);

2. entertainment and recreation (museums and galleries, casinos, concert and theater venues, gaming, parks, clubs, sports events, meeting and conferences and other attractions);

3. food and beverage (restaurants, fast foods, catering); and

4. travel and tourism (transportations, travel agencies, tour operations, airlines and cruise companies, guiding, visitors' information services).

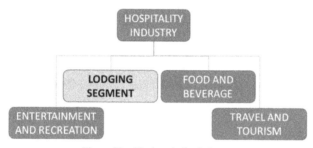

Figure 38 – The hospitality industry

According to the American Hotel and Lodging Educational Institute, the lodging segment has traditionally organized suppliers and customers according to well-established categoric instances.

While supplies are grouped according to eight criteria (level of service, target market, size, location, theme, ownership and affiliation, star rating and length of stay), the customers are classified as business, pleasure/leisure, group or international).

In the USA, the lodging guests share by use is: 29% for transient business travelers, 25% for attending conferences or group meetings, 24% on vacation and 21% for other purposes such as personal, family or special events.

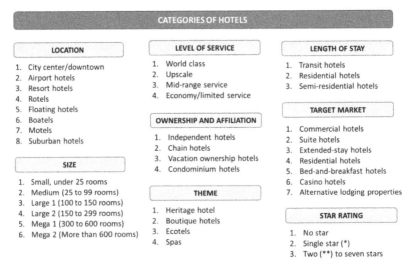

Figure 39 – Hotel categorization

⇨ Rotels [01], Floating hotels, Boatels, Vacation ownership hotels, Condominium hotels, Heritage hotel, Boutique hotels, Ecotels

## Target markets

The understanding of the target market categories will help to identify the value elements the incumbents deliver to their customers and, eventually support the value proposition adaptation required to react to the disrupter business (Airbnb).

As one facility can be simultaneously classified according to multiple features, I created a multi-dimensional hotel category viewer. To illustrate its application, I selected the Sheraton Hotel located in New York (Times Square).

According to its website (on July 28th, 2018),

*"with a stay at Sheraton New York Times Square Hotel, you'll be centrally located in New York, steps from Broadway Theatre and Ed Sullivan Theater. This 4-star hotel is close to Rockefeller Center and Broadway. It has 1780 air-conditioned rooms".*

Each lodging unit has a specific behavior which creates its own coverage shadow (as seen in the graph on the left).

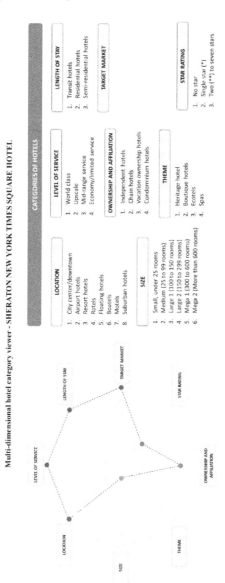

Figure 40 – Category viewer - Sheraton

In large hotel chains there are units with different and, above all, complementary coverage shadows meant to attract all types of customers. For example, only in the USA do Accor Hotels manage the following hotel brands:

RAFFLES  *Fairmont*  BANYAN TREE  LEGEN D  SO  SOFITEL  onefinestay

RIXOS  M  pullman  swissôtel  adagio  ANGSANA  25h twenty five hours hotels

MGallery  MAMA SHELTER  adagio  BreakFree  ibis  ibis styles  adagio

ibis budget  JO&JOE  hotelF1  Thalassa

Figure 41 – Accor Hotels

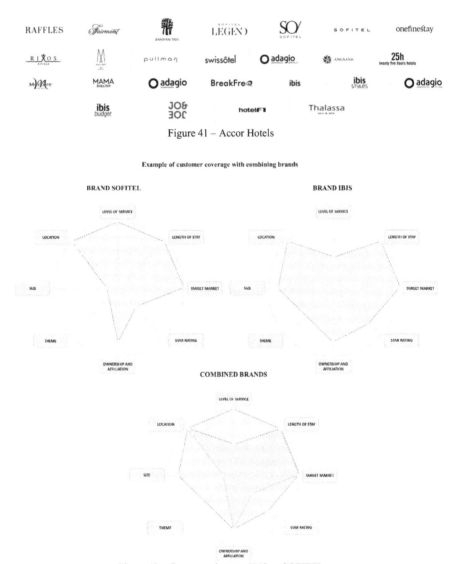

Figure 42 – Category viewer – IBIS vs SOFITEL

74

## The customer trajectory

Before addressing the disruptor business model, it is important to assess the features that influence the buyers' decision process. There are several elements to be considered:

- Satisfaction experience;
- Ads by a hotel or chain;
- Recommendations by family members and friends;
- Hotel location;
- Preconceptions of a hotel based on its name or affiliation;
- Travel management companies;
- How easy it is to make reservations;
- Hotel's quality of service, cleanliness and appearance;
- Loyalty to a particular property or brand;
- Frequent traveler program;
- Website design (for travelers documenting online).

---------------

Suggested reading

- Factors That Influence Customer Purchase Decisions by Larry Alton
- Selecting Online Travel Agencies by Edward Ku and Yi Wen Fan

-----------------

## The Airbnb characteristics

Considering the traditional buyers' influencers, the Airbnb model explores the following features underlined. Additionally, it explores the features in red.

When the Airbnb model is compared using the traditional categorization of hotels, some interesting information is revealed. The Airbnb accommodations are situated multiple locations, covering all traditional categories location and offering rooms in non-hotel districts. According to Camelon Digital Marketing 74% of Airbnb properties are outside the main hotel districts.

Airbnb is focused on economy/limited level of service and has no star rating. It also covers most of the scope of traditional hotels in terms of length of stay and target market – except for accommodations exclusively focused on high monetary value experiences.

Three features that have a differentiated experience from Airbnb are size, theme and ownership & affiliation. Despite the large number of available rooms on the Airbnb platform, most of them are in homes or in buildings smaller than any hotel traditional categorization.

**AIRBNB**

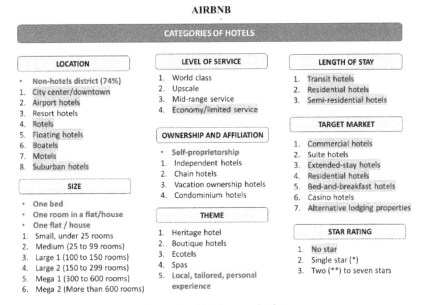

Figure 43 – Airbnb categorization

A relevant customer behavior is illustrated by the fact that, according to Airbnb, 91% of the customers want to live like a local and 79% wish to explore a specific neighborhood.

--------------------------------

Suggested reading

- 105 Airbnb Statistics and Facts by Craig Smith
- Airbnb Statistics for Demographics and Growth + more references
- About Us (Airbnb)
- How Airbnb Works | Insights into Business & Revenue Model

----------------------------------

**Inside-out trajectory**

Inside-out trajectory: *"These disruptions actually start by attacking a subset of your current customers as an incumbent. They get those customers first and then they start expanding out from that to take more and more of your customers"* Prof. David Rogers, during PGDDB.

The dynamics of Airbnb value proposition is structured upon five features: theme (A), ownership and affiliation (B), size (C), location (D) and level of service (E).

The value proposition of living like a local and exploring the neighborhood has five features:

- It was enabled by homeowners
- Homeowners offer accommodation in a new category of facility size, not considered in the traditional approach.
- It is done at budget prices.
- Approximately 74% of Airbnb properties are outside the main hotel districts.
- The level of service is below what is delivered even in small independent hotels.

**Multi-dimensional hotel category viewer – AIRBNB differentiation**

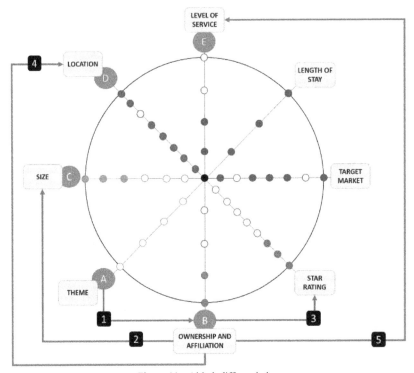

Figure 44 – Airbnb differentiation

The balance of these five features creates a value proposition that reaches most of the consumers in the traditional target markets; but cannot compete with the experiences offered in casino hotels, suite hotels, resorts or conference hotels.

On the other hand, Airbnb may offer a budget solution for people who want to go to a casino for a few days but who do not want to have high lodging expenses.

Finally, Airbnb may be offering a practical option to people that would not normally travel because of high accommodation costs or because they wish to explore regions that are not served by the traditional lodging sector. It is important to realize that this effect is not dependent on the hotel size. Therefore, it may affect low-cost unities, including up to three- star hotels.

On the other hand, Airbnb may offer a budget solution for people who want to go to a casino for a few days but who do not want to have high lodging expenses.

Finally, Airbnb may be offering a practical option to people that would not normally travel because of high accommodation costs or because they wish to explore regions that are not served by the traditional lodging sector. It is important to realize that this effect is not dependent on the hotel size. Therefore, it may affect low-cost unities, including up to three-star hotels.


## Outside-in trajectory

> Inside-out trajectory: *"So, it's starting outside of the realm of the customers of the incumbent, right? It starts outside your customer base, selling to someone else and then gradually as it gets better and it gets good enough, it starts moving in and attacking your customer base"* Prof. David Rogers, during PGDDB.

The Airbnb business model also offers a few mechanisms to produce an outside-in trajectory for customers. In fact, it is very likely the "outside-in trajectory" is the main revenue stream for Airbnb. According to Mahmoud, in his work The Impact of Airbnb on Hotel and Hospitality Industry, "each additional 10% increase in the size of the Airbnb market resulted in a 2-3 % decrease in hotel revenue". Therefore, 7% represents the potential outside-in trajectory".

- Low-income customers that may have first-time access to the lodging structure in touristic areas
- Regular travelers that will extend their stay (from commercial hotel value proposition to extended-stay)
- Travelers who wish to visit non-hotel districts
- Low-budget travelers happy to share a room
- Alternative lodging property users (recreational vehicle parks, campgrounds, mobile home parks) who value living the local experience

## Scope of customer loss

A few facts must be considered:

1. The global hotel industry revenue is estimated at US$ 570bi (2016).

2. In the same period the top 50 global hotel chains have an estimated annual revenue of US$ 40 billion (7% of global lodging sector).

3. Item 2 suggests a significant part of this industry revenue is generated in small chains, in independent hotels or in small lodging facilities.

4. According to the American Hotel and Lodging Association, in the USA 60% of hotels are small businesses, which confirms Item 3 above.

5. Despite the fact Airbnb claims 81% of hosts share the home in which they live, according to CBRE "true home-sharing, where the owner is present during the guest's stay, accounts for less than 20% of Airbnb's business. 81% of Airbnb's revenue nationwide comes from whole-unit rentals where the owner is not present."

6. Items 2, 4 and 5 suggest that Airbnb tends to affect small lodging solutions more than large hotel chains businesses. Except, eventually, for low-cost brands of these hotel chains.

7. Most affected businesses are bed & breakfast hotels, inns, motels and pensions. On the other hand, these businesses have joined the Airbnb platform and, together with the guest houses, form the new disruptive ecosystem.

This sequence of facts show that the Airbnb platform aggregates several small lodging businesses, located everywhere, to offer economy and mid-range service, for different lengths of stay, at a lower cost, without several amenities usually offered by large hotel chains (such as room service, laundry/valet service, concierge service, in-room refreshment services, pools, saunas, etc.).

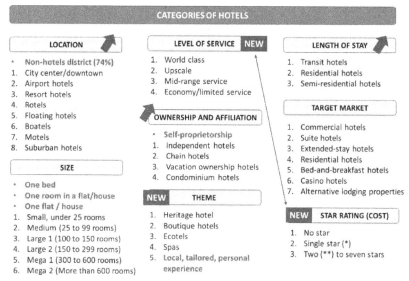

Figure 45 – Scope of customer loss

------------------

Suggested reading

Hosts with Multiple Units -- A Key Driver of Airbnb Growth

------------------

Airbnb value proposition is based on a new cost-benefit balance (lower cost, less benefits) and a new theme (living like a local) while enhancing the traditional values of location (anywhere), length of stay (stay longer as it is cheaper) and ownership and affiliation (as Airbnb offers a strong brand to the smaller businesses that exist on the platform).

The value of size seems to be irrelevant to the average targeted customer. This value proposition and the digital platform ecosystem creates a business and a brand that targets the markets occupied by customers that look for budget solutions in commercial hotels, extended-stay hotels and residential hotels.

## Airbnb primary focus

Based on the scenario illustrated in the previous sections, it can be said that Airbnb is primarily focusing on customers who are travelling on vacation or because of other personal reasons. A secondary customer is the transient business travelers. Those people traveling to large conferences or group meetings are not targeted by Airbnb.

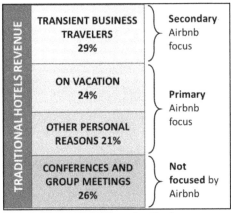

Figure 46 - My incumbent business

## Wyndham Hotels and Resorts

Wyndham Hotels and Resorts is an international hotel and resort chain based in the United States – Airbnb´s largest market. It has locations in Canada, Mexico, Colombia, Ecuador, Turkey, Germany, the UK, the Caribbean and Margarita Island in Venezuela.

The seventh most valuable hotel brand in the world (Hotel Management, Feb,2018), Wyndham organized its hotels in eight categories:

- Destinations (Club Wyndham, Shell Vacation Club, Margarita Ville, Cottages.com, Landal, Wyndham Vacations Rental, WorldMark);

82

- Caesars Entertainments (Caesars, Harrah's, Horseshoe, The Cromwell, Bally's, Flamingo, The Link, Nobu Hotel, Paris, Planet Hollywood, Rio);

- Distinctive (Wyndham Grand);

- Upscale (Dolce, Wyndham);

- Lifestyle (Tryp, Explendor, Dazzler, TradeMark);

- Midscale (LQHotel, Wingate, Wyndham Garden, AmericInn, Ramada, Encore);

- Value (Microtel, Days Inn, Super 8, Howard Johnson, Travelodge);

- Extended stay (Hawthorn).

The category most sensitive to the growth of Airbnb is the "value" with its five brands:

- Microtel: *"we know you've got a busy schedule. Whether you're gearing up for back-to-back meetings or need time to relax and unwind, what you want from your hotel is a consistent, seamless stay"* [01]. Being focused on business travelers, Microtel is not a primary focus for Airbnb.

- Super 8: *"With style and comfort in mind, our redesigned guest rooms make Super 8 your reliable roadside companion."* Considering the primary revenue streams for Airbnb are in populated urban areas (despite the fact that most of the accommodations are in non-hotel districts), Super 8 is not a primary focus for Airbnb.

- Travellodge: *"The difference between a trip and an adventure? The can-do, can-conquer attitude than can only come from a good night's sleep. Whether it's a sandy beach, a bustling downtown or a hike in one of our national parks - every great adventure starts with a great night's sleep. Get up + GO."* Again, considering the primary revenue streams for Airbnb are in populated urban areas, Travellodge is not a primary focus for Airbnb.

## Top 10 Most Valuable Brands

**Hilton** — **1**
Rank 2018: **1**  2017: **1**  →
BV 2018: **$6,330m**  -24%
BV 2017: **$8,370m**
Brand Rating: **AAA-**

**Marriott** — **2**
Rank 2018: **2**  2017: **2**  →
BV 2018: **$5,464m**  +8%
BV 2017: **$5,037m**
Brand Rating: **AAA-**

**HYATT** — **3**
Rank 2018: **3**  2017: **3**  →
BV 2018: **$3,512m**  -13%
BV 2017: **$4,037m**
Brand Rating: **AA+**

**Holiday Inn** — **4**
Rank 2018: **4**  2017: **5**  ↑
BV 2018: **$3,292m**  +8%
BV 2017: **$3,044m**
Brand Rating: **AAA**

**COURTYARD Marriott** — **5**
Rank 2018: **5**  2017: **6**  ↑
BV 2018: **$3,018m**  +25%
BV 2017: **$2,421m**
Brand Rating: **AAA-**

**SHANGRI-LA** — **6**
Rank 2018: **6**  2017: **9**  ↑
BV 2018: **$2,221m**  +35%
BV 2017: **$1,650m**
Brand Rating: **AAA-**

**WYNDHAM** — **7**
Rank 2018: **7**  2017: **11**  ↑
BV 2018: **$1,976m**  +32%
BV 2017: **$1,492m**
Brand Rating: **AAA-**

**Sheraton** — **8**
Rank 2018: **8**  2017: **4**  ↓
BV 2018: **$1,902m**  -50%
BV 2017: **$3,819m**
Brand Rating: **AAA-**

**RAMADA** — **9**
Rank 2018: **9**  2017: **8**  ↓
BV 2018: **$1,890m**  +13%
BV 2017: **$1,676m**
Brand Rating: **AA+**

**Hampton** — **10**
Rank 2018: **10**  2017: **7**  ↓
BV 2018: **$1,784m**  -23%
BV 2017: **$2,306m**
Brand Rating: **AAA-**

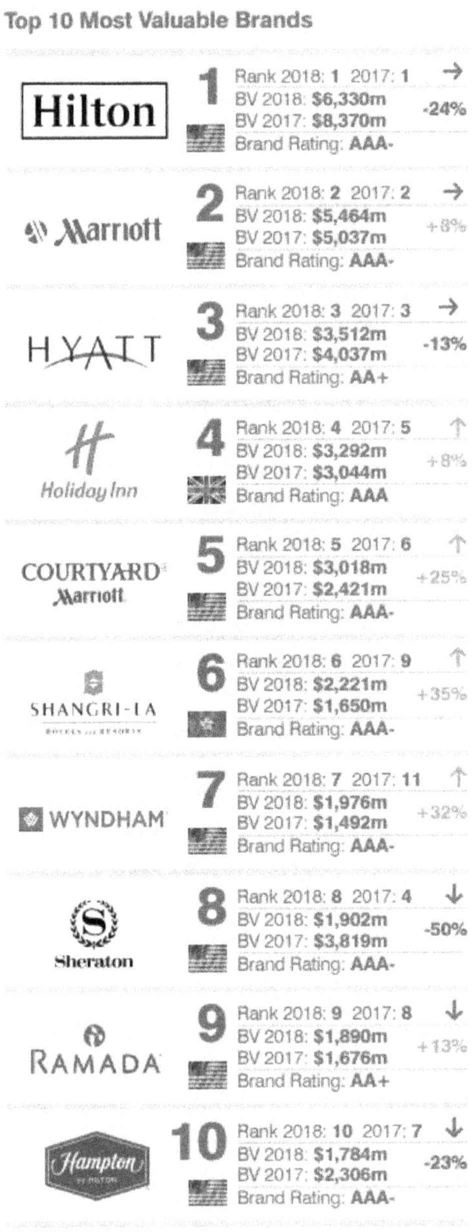

Figure 47 – Most valuable brands

84

- Howard Johnson: *"You can count on us when your family wants to take a trip without feeling like they've gone too far from home. It's the same warm, friendly experience we've offered for decades - because we know that honest hospitality never goes out of style."*[i] This brand is a target for Airbnb.

- Days Inn: *"it's always go-time at Days Inn. Days Inn morning fuel includes fresh fruit, yogurts, cereals, oatmeal, juice and coffee. Most of our hotels include a fitness center or pool. Most Days Inn hotels provide free WiFi, plus some offer restaurants, bars and meeting space to round out holistically-healthy and productive stays."* This brand is a target for Airbnb.

Therefore, the Howard Johnson Hotels and the Days Inn Hotels are the Wyndham Hotel chain brands that have a value proposition similar to Airbnb.

According to Statista, the Wyndham total revenue in 2017 was US$ 5bi [01]. But according to CSIMarket, the lodging operation responds for 23% of Wyndham Hotels total revenue (or US$ 1.2 billion), while Vacation Exchange Rental contributes with 30% and Vacation Ownership 47% (CSI Market)

According to Wyndham Worldwide Reports Fourth Quarter and Full-Year 2017 Results, the brands Howard Johnson and Days Inn generated US$ 5.7 million revenue – 47% of lodging operation and 11% of Wyndham's group.

Despite the revenue reduction in the Wyndham's group (from US$ 5.6 bi to US$ 5.1 bi), the lodging operations delivered 2.6% growth (2017 vs 2016). This result (+2.6%) is the average variation of 16 brands (Super 8, Days Inn, Rama-da, Wyndham Hotels and Resorts, Howard Johnson, Baymont, Travelodge, Microtel Inns & Suites, Knights Inn, TRYP, Wingate, Hawthorn Suites, Dolce, Dazzler and Esplendor).

Considering that Howard Johnson and Days Inn are the brands more exposed to Airbnb competition, it is very likely its revenue has decreased. However, there is no public information about this.

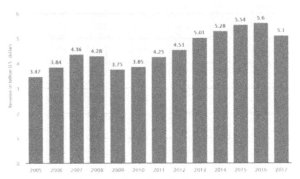

Figure 48 – Wyndham total revenue

Given that these two brands account for 11% of the group's revenue and 47% of the lodging operations revenue, it is fair to think of mechanisms to protect these businesses from Airbnb competition.

**Disrupter: niche, splitting or total takeover?**

Airbnb is currently offering a value proposition that focuses on a specific niche of the lodging industry. The disruptor (Airbnb) competes in a segment that represents 11% of the incumbent (Wyndham) market size. Additionally, as mentioned, up to 70% of Airbnb's customers have an outside-in trajectory while less than 30# are inside-out.

In 2017, Airbnb made US$ 2.6 bi in revenue. Given that they receive an average of 10% of the documenting fees, it is fair to say that Airbnb is accountable for nearly US$ 26 bi of the hotel industry – that represents 4.4% of the global lodging sector revenue.

The growth seen in these first eight years increases the possibility that Airbnb will split the market into two major categories: economy and non-economy. Although this seems to be unlikely now, the competitors – particularly the large hotel chains – need to properly react now to avoid this scenario.

## Other incumbent industries

As described, the hospitality industry has four main sectors:

- lodging segment (hotels, inns, motels, pensions, resorts, bed & break-fasts, villas and cottages, guest houses.);

- entertainment and recreation (museums and galleries, casinos, concert and theater venues, gaming, parks, clubs, sports events, meeting and conferences and other attractions);

- food and beverage (restaurants, fast foods, catering); and

- travel and tourism (transportations, travel agencies, tour operations, airlines and cruise companies, guiding, visitors' information services).

As Airbnb is directly influencing the Path-to-Purchase, it disrupts by changing the dynamics within the DISTRIBUTOR train. Initially, the competition occurred in relation to the lodging segment (1) but the digital platform already offers solutions that compete with the entertainment and recreations sector (2) and with the travel and tourism sector (4).

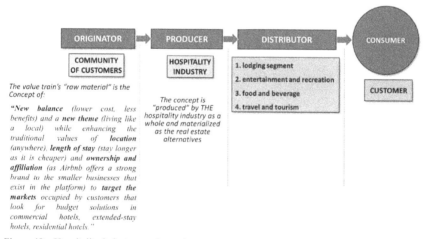

Figure 49 – Hospitality industry – value train

Therefore, it is very likely that companies such as museums and galleries, casinos, concert and theater venues, parks, clubs, sports events, transportations, travel agencies, tour operations, airlines and cruise companies, guiding, visitors' information services need to be part of the Airbnb platform in the future to avoid losing money. In fact, the travel and tourism sector itself is already under disruption because of the effect that digital companies try to implement pure digital models to disintermediate the entire process, provide extremely better customer experience and barrier competition.

## Disruptive response planner

We need to look at the different variables that define the different cases of disruptive business models. First, we showed that the customer trajectory occurs in both ways: inside-out and outside-in. Both are significant movements, although I understand outside-in accounts for two thirds of Airbnb revenue.

The second point is to evaluate how much of the customer base Airbnb is likely to threaten or challenge. As explained, in the case of Wyndham Hotels, in the short time 11% of the revenue is generated by brands with a value proposition that can be threatened by Airbnb. Although it is not the main revenue source, it is big enough to fight for.

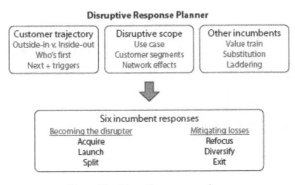

Figure 50 – Disruptive response planner

The third point is associated to the network effects. The Airbnb business model is structured based on a digital platform where consumers interact with suppliers (home owners and small businesses). Since its startup in 2010, Airbnb increased its annual revenue to US$ 2.6 bi, producing customers´ expenses estimated at US$ 26 bi which is 4.4% of the global lodging sector.

Its market value is now higher than any other traditional hotel chain. Largely sustained on the massification of its network effect, "the growth seen in these first eight years increases the possibility that Airbnb will split the market into two major categories: economy and non-economy". This is now an unlikely possibility that cannot be neglected by the incumbents.

**This scenario exposes several other incumbents to disruption:**

- Other low-cost hotel brands in large Hotel chains such as Hilton Worldwide Holdings, Marriott International, Hyatt Hotels Corp, Starwood Hotels and Resorts, Intercontinental Hotels Group, Accor, Shangri-La Asia, Whitbread Plc, etc.

- Small and medium size independent hotels that cannot meet the lower cost-fewer service level balance suggested by Airbnb – and this represents a very high share of the hotel sector

- The entertainment and recreation firms that have operational agreements with traditional hotel chains to offer activities in museums, galleries, casinos, concert and theater venues, gaming, parks, clubs, sports events, etc. to their guests. The Airbnb recommending tools and online content may reduce the revenue of these firms – largely based on a disintermediation process. In this case, disintermediation has already happened. For these companies, the risk is not to be part of the Airbnb ecosystem.

- The food and beverage (restaurants, fast foods, catering) industry created to supply vending machines, bars and restaurants in the targeted hotel brands will be affected as Airbnb guests will get their food elsewhere;

- The travel and tourism (transportation, travel agencies, tour operators, airlines and cruise companies, guiding, visitors' information services). In this case, disintermediation has already happened. For these companies, the risk is not to be part of the Airbnb ecosystem.

When we look at the value chain, it is likely that hotel chains and small and medium independent hotels will be affected by Airbnb. On the other hand, the food and beverage sectors are more exposed to competition and substitution.

Finally, for the entertainment and recreation sector and for the travel and tourism sector, the laddering process is a better fit to explain Airbnb impact as the why-why analysis leads to a movement towards becoming a stakeholder on the digital platform.

**Symmetric competitors – affected incumbents**

Before addressing the six incumbents responses, let´s look at what other incumbents (symmetric competitors) have done to react to Airbnb influence.

Marriott: the Moxy Hotels were first launched in Milan in 2014 targeting the millennial customers. Today it has 26 open properties (81 in the pipeline).

> *"Ready for a good time? Moxy Hotels makes that easy with the heart of a boutique hotel and an appetite for adventure. There's a drink waiting for you with your room key and someone at the bar that wants your number. Moxy is for play... Jenga, karaoke, maybe a little game of spin the bottle? Here, you can get away with it. Our lobbies are like living rooms with a bartender. Our guest rooms are like a cozy clubhouse you never want to leave, where you curl up in soft sheets, stream your favorite movie from our white-hot WiFi and cocoon for as long as you want. Because we want you to have it all."*

IHG: To strengthen its customer relationship, IHG enhanced its loyalty program and in 2015 launched a series of mobile and in-hotel digital technology pilots for check-in, check-out, bill conference, room key, guest request and customized recommendations.

Sheraton: in 2015 Sheraton unveiled a comprehensive 10-point plan [Hotel News Now] designed to put Sheraton Hotels and Resorts firmly back into the global spotlight. It includes:

- new brand positioning to enhance the digital experience;

- rolling out a multichannel global advertising campaign to ramp up media buzz and social strategy into meaningfully engage consumers across all channels; and

- creating a flexible new-build product that enhances hotel profitability in secondary and tertiary markets.

**Airbnb competitors**

Their most visible Airbnb competitor is HomeAway. Digital customers have had several debates on the strengths and weaknesses of these brands. Here is the example of HomeAway:

HomeAway: according to its website, HomeAway, a world leader in the vacation rental industry, is the place to document beach houses, cabins and condos with more than two million places to stay in 190 countries.

HomeAway, Inc. was founded in 2005 and in 2015 was acquired by Expedia for $3.9 billion. HomeAway operates more than 50 websites in 23 languages with rentals in 190 countries. The average traveler is a 35-to-50-year-old female who travels with family, typically a group of four or more people.

Vacation and special occasions are the most common reasons for a trip, with an average stay of seven days. After staying in a vacation rental for the first time, 82% of travelers plan to do so again in the future. By renting a vacation home, many travelers can get twice the space for half the cost of a hotel.

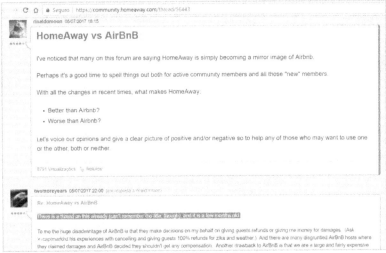

Figure 51 – Airbnb competitors

But there are many other smaller companies competing in this market. The website "The Choosy Traveler" published an article in entitled "14 Airbnb alternatives 2019: the best websites like Airbnb for an awesome getaway" that compare features such as rental locations, documenting fees charging policies and type of accommodation (budget, mid-range, luxury). The list includes the following companies: Homestay.com, Flipkey, Couchsurfing, Love Home, Plans Matter, Booking.com, Kid & Coe, Wimdu, BedyCasa, OneFineStay, HomeEscape, 9Flats.com, Casamundo, Trusted Housesitters.

I would recommend that Wyndham acquires one of the Airbnb competitors. First because making acquisitions, it is aligned with its culture. For example, in May 2018 Wyndham acquired La Quinta Holdings (900 hotels and 89,000 rooms) for almost US$ 2 billion.

Secondly, with an acquisition, Wyndham Hotels will accelerate the learning curve and promote a quicker response to Airbnb expansion. This approach excludes the option for launching an independent disrupter. Thirdly, the acquisition of its own digital platform will enable Wyndham to promote other types of responses: diversification.

The diversification of its portfolio including the know-how to offer complementary services identified in the DISTRIBUTOR train will strengthen the group's position in relation to Airbnb's value proposition. Note the recommendation is not associated to controlling the companies that offer these services, but controlling the ecosystem other companies operate in. By adopting this strategy, Wyndham would reject the possibility of splitting the disrupter's business model with other incumbents.

The share of the business threatened by Airbnb (11%) is high enough to eliminate any plan for fast exit. The strategy of refocus on defensible customers is not required as the lodging industry naturally has a very segmented management strategy and the brands not directly affected by Airbnb are well cared for.

The recommendation relies on acquiring a disrupter and then diversifying the portfolio of services offered.

# Media Industry Case Study

## 5. Media industry: data strategy

### The newspaper business

This case study explores the operation of São Paulo Distribuição e Logistica (SPDL), a logistics provider founded in 2002 as a partnership of the two of the largest newspaper publishing groups in Brazil (Estado SP, 1875 and Folha de SP, 1921).

Figure 52 – The Brazilian newspapers: "O Estado de S. Paulo" and "Folha de São Paulo"

SPDL delivers newspapers to 4,200 newsstands and to 216,000 subscribers in 115,000 locations in the São Paulo Metropolitan Region. SPDL was created to reduce costs through the synergy of the pre-existing assets of the founding groups, as they had similar delivery itineraries.

Today the newspapers are produced in two printing facilities (one for each founding group) and transported to four distribution centers (DCs) where they are prepared for transportation to the consumers.

94

Figure 53 – Area of influence

There is a tight delivery window to perform this operation. The first hour is used for handling the newspapers (assembling the distinct parts that are printed separately, manually inserting advertisements and putting them in bags) and the other 3 hours are dedicated to delivering the product to the customers.

Figure 54 – User experience cycle

More recently, the two companies have been facing drops in circulation and loss of revenue from classified advertising, putting more pressure on their costs; not to mention soaring real estate costs that impact the rental/lease cost of their distribution centers and the worsening in traffic congestion that affects the productivity of the vehicles.

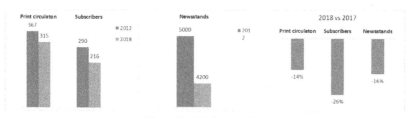

Figure 55 – Business results

The company performs network design analysis to simulate different optimized distribution operations with improved cost-efficiency while ensuring the service level. The studies include

(i) centralization vs. decentralization of the distribution centers;

(ii) centralization of handling activities at the printing sites

(iii) sharing the printing of newspapers of the founding groups in both printing sites;

(iv) late delivery of the newspapers to customers located in more distant peripheral regions.

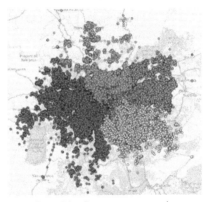

Figure 56 – Customer segmentation

Recently, it was decided to close one DC and change the type of vehicles used to collect the newspapers at the printing sites. The fleet of vehicles and personnel used in the final delivery operations was adjusted (+5% motorcycles; - 80% van assistants; -17% vans.

The number of managers, coordinators, leaders, supervisors, administration assistants and young apprentices was also reduced. This yielded to a cost reduction of the collecting freight cost of 18%.

## Using data

As a reaction to the reduction of circulation and loss of revenue from classified advertising, the Media Group is using distribution operations data to optimize costs and recover margin contributions. Although necessary, this strategy is neither enough nor the most effective in the long run.

There is an opportunity for this company to use data strategically to generate revenue and achieve complementary cost reductions. Today, "business process data is used to manage and optimize business operations". There are three opportunities:

- More effective use of business process data to achieve further cost reductions and generate revenue;

- Using product and service data to create new revenue channels;

- Using customer data to "provide a complete picture of the customer and allow for more relevant and valuable interactions".

Additionally, it is important to mention that digital transformation is less associated to designing a new business model that prepares the company for the future and more focused on providing the same information in different channels (printed version, mobile and PC).

An example of this strategy is illustrated in Figure 57. The picture was taken at my home on June 9th, 2018. The same information can be accessed in three different ways. It should be mentioned that I am a subscriber who receives the printed version only on Saturdays and Sundays and have online access 24/7.

Therefore, it is important to move from using limited business process data to an environment where product, service and customer data are strategically available to enable the creation of new revenue streams.

97

Figure 57 – Different media

Therefore, it is important to move from using limited business process data to an environment where product, service and customer data are strategically available to enable the creation of new revenue streams.

**Path-to-purchase**

---------------------

Suggested reading

Path to Purchase: Understanding the Customer Journey by James Lovejoy

---------------------

As introduced, the media group that controls the two biggest newspapers in Brazil are focusing on cost reduction based on the use of process data enabling operational efficiency gains.

The efforts to map the operations are constant and the visibility of internal operations (editing, printing and assembling) and external operations (delivery) has been consistent and intense over the last years.

Despite these efforts, last mile data lacks accuracy as there is no mechanism to track delivery routing execution. Different tracking technologies were evaluated but neither costs or security constraints inhibited its implementation.

98

This initiative would evolve the coordination of people, devices and technologies. Again, the cost of implementation seems to be prohibitive given the scale of operations and the quantity of devices required.

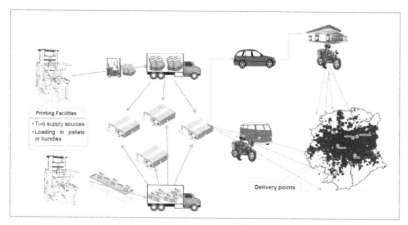

Figure 58 – The logistics

The existing approach to data management offers a very limited understanding of the business given that it neglects the consumer user experience. Today, this media group captures and monitors data generated during the delivery operations from 2:30 to 6:30am and registers the costs associated to the other operations and administrative activities (including the editing phase). The customers reading cycle, from 6:30am to 11:00pm produces no relevant data.

Figure 59 – User experience cycle (b)

As long as the media group that controls SPDL and newspaper operations does not capture the data associated to the consumer experience cycle, it will not

99

understand the entire path-to-purchase and no strategy will be able to create differentiated value to customers and business. The opportunity I see, therefore, is associated to understanding user behavior and interacting with them in an unseen way.

## How to capture data on customer behavior

The use of QR (Quick Response) codes is common in print advertising, magazines advert, flyers, posters, invites, TV ads and even in newspapers, containing: product details, contact details, offer details, event details, competition details, Twitter / Facebook / MySpace IDs, a link to their YouTube video, etc. [01]

-----------------------------------

Suggested reading

### What is a social media ID?

- 10 Advantages and disadvantages of social logins
- Social Login - Time to implement it in your apps
- Prevent social media ID theft

-----------------------------------

According to the Search Engine Land, the reason "why they are more useful than a standard barcode is that they can store (and digitally present) much more data, including URL links, geo coordinates, and text.

Figure 60 – Use of QR Code - Ralph Lauren

100

The other key feature of QR Codes is that instead of requiring a chunky hand-held scanner to scan them, many modern cell phones can scan them.

Using QR codes in newspapers is not recent. In 2011 the Spring River Chronicle announced the use of QR codes. According to the site Editor & Publisher, "it may be unexpected that the Spring River Chronicle, a 3,000-circulation weekly paper published in Hardy, Ark. (population 756), would be one of the pioneers to embrace this new technology trend, but Jody Shackelford is not the average newspaper publisher.

The 25-year-old started his first publication — a regional magazine — at the age of 22. While most entrepreneurs his age are in search of the next big online idea, Shackelford chose to venture into the newspaper industry earlier this year in order to test a new concept — a print newspaper that reads the stories to you."

Figure 61 – QR Core – example (b)

Shackelford said that they "took QR codes beyond advertising and now deliver full audio versions of articles via QR codes directly from the headlines," so that "readers can scan and listen to the newspaper, word for word, while they drive to work or wash the car. They can listen anytime, anywhere."

Later in January 2012, the USA Today allowed their readers to launch interactive content using a QR code and a smartphone. They worked together with AT&T to bring these "mobile barcodes" to the newspaper-reading public.

Figure 62 – USA Today

The newspaper decided to have the codes in every section while the AT&T codes bridged "the gap between purely digital content and the traditional printed word". According to the site Shake the Tech, the newspaper "will be able to judge more what their readership is interested in". Still according to the same website, "the information age passed up the traditional channels of information putting many of them, the newspapers, out of business. The USA Today strategy is attempting to put a cap on that trend."

Figure 63 – USA Today - Strategy

In "Grupo Folha" and "Grupo Estado", the media conglomerates that own the two biggest Brazilian newspapers, the use of QR code is a reality.

It is used to enable the reader of the printed version to access the same information as on the smartphone. There is a section "Corrida", one page where the news information of the last seven days is summarized - there are sometimes QR codes for some of this news. However, on June 6th, 2018 for example, there was no QR code in the entire printed version I received at home.

Figure 64 – QR Code – Example (e)

Today the number of QR code suppliers (such as QFuse) for publishers is increasing and the applications may be relevant for different situations such as those brainstormed by Chris Snider in his blog:

- Ask a "question of the day" in print (a lot of sports sections do this already), and let readers see the answer by scanning the QR code;

- Link to the correct answers to today's crossword puzzle;

- Link to expanded box scores in your sports agate;

- Allow readers to enter a contest; Put one on the side of a bus.

- Or on an ad inside a bus (or subway); Put them on your newspaper racks – on street corners and in stores; Put QR codes in advertisements; Have a QR code that users can scan in to send breaking news to the newsroom; Allow readers to sign up for breaking news text alerts; Put one with a story so readers can easily share the story with friends.

Another application for QR codes comes from The Daily Jang, a 75-year-old newspaper brand in Pakistan. According to the blog of the World Association of Newspapers and News Publishers, The Jang "has introduced (in 2016) QR codes in its printed classified ads, allowing readers to access additional information about advertised products by scanning the codes with their smartphones".

103

Figure 65 – QR Code provider

Anton Jolkovski writes that The Jang claims a 50-percent share of readership in the country and a 70-percent share of the classifieds market. He explains that "the newspaper classified advertisers request the QR feature at the time of documenting. They receive a unique code via SMS on the mobile number they used to register the classified ad.

They use the code to log on to the Jang QR classified website, where they can upload photos and videos related to their advertisement". On the other hand, the readers "can use any QR reader app on their smartphones to scan the code and see pictures and videos of the automobile and property that is being advertised".

Figure 66 - World Association of Newspapers and News Publishers

"Jang has long been the leader and most trusted classified source for customers for decades. With this major innovation and development, Jang has clearly shown it is the classified leader and is going to stay there for a long time to come," he said.

According to QFuse feature summary, the QR codes provide a number of solutions to publishers, such as: advanced QR code scan analytics, mobile landing pages & micro-sites, QR code & NFC Tag management, video & photos, social media & social sharing, interactive contacts at-a-touch, NFC compatible, mapping & GPS, mobile commerce, mobile lead capture and specials, subscriptions & promotions.

-----------------

Suggested reading

- QR Code Metrics: How do you monitor QR code results?
- How to Track QR Codes with Google Analytics by Suzanne Trevellyan
- QR Code Tracking & Analytics
- Mobile Landing Page Best Practices by Jacinda Santora
- What the Hell Is a Microsite and Why Do I Need One? by Melissa Lafsky
- The Best Microsite Examples We've Ever Seen by Lindsay Kolowich
- Social sharing with QR codes by Jeff Korhan
- How To Use QR Codes In Social Media by Greg Finn
- NFC Compatibility
- 5 Lead Capture Apps You Need To Know About
- Mobile Lead Capture

--------------------

This section aims to clarify that the use of QR codes is already popular and proven in the publishing sector. The cost to print each QR code is insignificant when compared to any tracking device SPDL has tested to capture data from delivery operations.

Even cheaper solutions such as smart tags (electronic product code) (see examples) would cost from US 0.08/unit, which is a significant value when multiplied for the volume or compared to the newspaper selling price. For example, the selling revenue generated from SPDL newspapers equals the total operational costs (from editing to delivering), while the profit comes from publicity revenue, which has also reduced during recent years.

The challenge is to identify how to use this existing solution (QR code) in a traditional sector (printed newspapers) to generate strategic data capable to initiate a business turnaround and boost new revenue streams. The goal of this case is to suggest how data, as an asset, can support a new business model capable of assuring long term success to these publishing conglomerates.

### Managing data as a strategic asset

The planned use of QR codes, thought to capture strategic data for business, may have complementary utilities, as illustrated in this section. The idea is to associate a QR code to most articles of each section and incentive the readers to "read" the codes with their smartphones and interact in different ways.

### Business process data

Some interactions will contribute as business process data. The basic data generation protocol associates the QR code "reading event" to the consumer, the time of day and the location of the consumer. This basic information will provide accurate information on when and where the consumer actually reads the newspaper for the first time.

For example, if SPDL delivers a newspaper at 8am in the consumer's office, it may be more cost-effective than delivering it at 6am at his home. The possibility of having a delivery address different from the consumer's home address is a potential benefit for reducing overall distribution costs.

| Data Type & Utility | |
|---|---|
| A. Business process data | Applications |
| Manage & optimize business operations, reduce risk, provide external reporting | A1. Basic information |
| | A2. Day-long experience |
| | A3. Where/when newspaper is disposed of in the trash |

Figure 67 - Business process data

This initial feature also allows the media group to understand the consumer experience during the day and associate the reading activities to specific periods of the day. Consumers that only start reading their newspaper at lunchtime may be offered discounted prices for late delivery service.

This strategy can reduce the total assets required for distribution (motorcycles, vans and personnel) as their use could be extended during the entire morning.

A third business process data application regards the destination of the product after its one-day life cycle. The destination of this huge quantity of paper is an environmental issue.

A QR code to be associated to the moment and location the user is throwing the newspaper away is quite relevant. This may occur on the same day it was delivered or many weeks afterwards, in the case where the consumer keeps old newspapers for various domestic purposes.

Regardless of the lifecycle time, the location and the moment the newspaper is discharged is relevant as it may help the company to create mechanisms for more environmentally friendly operations.

**Product or service data**

The QR codes provide options to interact with the consumer and generate product or service-related data about the newspaper. For example, the publisher can evaluate which photographer has more positive or negative feedbacks.

107

| Data Type & Utility | Examples |
|---|---|
| B. Product or service data | |
| Deliver the core value proposition of the business product or service | B1. Reporters & Photographers |
| | B2. Comments & Reviews |
| | B3. Theme & sections |
| | B4. Figures, graphs, pictures |
| | B5. Long vs. short |

Figure 68 - Product or service data

A deeper analysis will indicate what attributes in a photo make a better impression on consumers. Depending on specific characteristics, such as age, gender or localizations, some consumers may prefer to see real people in the images while others prefer landscapes. The analysis may perceive the differences when comparing feedback from mobile Apps, PCs and printed versions. This information will enhance the quality of the user's experience as specific guidelines may be adopted for specific sections of the newspaper.

The same approach can be used to capture data on consumer preferences by letting the consumers (readers) comment or review news, publicity, special documents. The data generated enables the publisher to improve customer experience based on preferences related to themes or sections, quality, format or content of figures, graphs and pictures and the length of the news.

From the personnel perspective, all this product-related information enables corporate orientation on how or what to include in each edition. Therefore, reporters, photographers, editors and all staff will be able to dedicate efforts in a customer-driven environment. A change in the culture and mindset will reinforce brand loyalty and reduce the speed readers are abandoning the printed version of the newspaper.

**Consumer data**

The QR codes provide a variety of options to interact with the consumer to generate product or service improvements. A loyalty program may be the incentive to keep readers interacting with the various QR codes printed in the newspapers. The loyalty program design is not addressed in this case.

Figure 69 - Consumer macro-moments (Original Link)

The ability to associate the reading event to specific locations can identify "reading channels" such as cafeterias, shopping centers, public parks, commercial buildings, etc. For example, if the reader has just read a text on Paris, the media group may suggest complementary news on Paris (France) or Europe.

A more detailed solution may associate this reader to hotel or flights documenting services – in order not to be too invasive, it is possible to adjust a setup option in the reader profile where he/she indicates if he/she wishes to be informed about these services.

| Data Type & Utility | Examples |
|---|---|
| C. Customer data | |
| Provide a complete picture of the customer and allow for more relevant and valuable interactions | C1. Reward vs links |
| | C2. Quantity vs daytime |
| | C3. Time in the day |
| | C4. Reading channels |
| | C5. Age, Gender, Profession |
| | C6. Location |
| | C7. Days of the week |
| | C8. Charge publicity |
| | C9. Total time |

Figure 70 - Customer data

The data on age, gender, profession, location and days of the week will produce quality big data capable of enhancing overall customer experience and producing complementary revenue channels with a multiservice environment (hotels, flights, and any other product or service related to a specific journal section).

In another example, when discussing the economy, the publisher may generate a survey on the bank sector brand equity – this would provide better arguments to negotiate specific publicity fees with the banking sector.

With all this data regarding customer behavior, it is possible to understand the total reading time per consumer, per day, per section, per age, etc. These metrics can anticipate the increase in the churn rate and, therefore, allow the planning of customized actions based on consumers' behavior.

## Five core behaviors of customers

The suggested data management strategy will impact the relationship with readers. I have observed this impact according to a customer network perspective, using the five core behaviors of customers. Despite the fact this is a qualitative and quick analysis, it can be observed that the proposed data management has the potential to impact the relationship with consumers in a very significant way.

Figure 66 illustrates the potential impact intensity of the strategic use of the data collected from the interaction between consumers and the QR codes printed in the newspapers. The capacity to produce content considering the preference attributes captured from consumers will reduce the churn rate as it is expected that word-of-mouth incentives have a higher access.

Despite the fact the concept of "ACCESS" is related to "be faster, easier, more on-demand" – which is not the case in this business, I would emphasize this point as it would represent a turnaround in relation to the subscription's reduction trend in recent years.

| 5 digital consumer behaviors | The indirect impact of data gathering. The consequences of using the data captured |
|---|---|
| Access (be faster, easier, more on-demand): | Reduction of churn rate |
| Engage (be a source of valued content): | High Impact |
| Customize (be adaptable to different customer needs): | High Impact |
| Connect (be a valuable part of customers' online and social conversations): | Small Impact |
| Collaborate (invite customers to help build your business and your enterprise): | High Impact |

Figure 71 - Five core behaviors

111

The first relevant behavior is COLLABORATION. Each interaction via QR code is an input to improve the quality of the service (relevance of information) and the quality of the product (layout of the news, photos, graphs… in the news-paper). As consequence, the media group can customize the content and, therefore, increase customer engagement.

---------------

Suggested reading

Digital Transformation in News Media, by M. Friedrichsen and Y. Kamalipour

------------------

# SAP Case Study

## 6. ERP systems: industry transformation

### The ERP System Business

*"ERP (Enterprise Resource Planning) is business procedure managing soft-ware that allows business to use integrated ap-plication for a system to run business. It also computerized various back office tasks associated to technol-ogy, HR and services, such as project planning, managing HR, accounting and financial applications, reducing redundant tasks, distribution process manage-ment, improving accuracy of financial data and more. Enterprise resource planning software combines all features of a business such as planning, manu-facturing, retailing and selling."* (MarketWatch)

Some of the leading ERP manufacturers are Oracle, IBM, Microsoft, SAP, Infor, Sage, Netsuite, Totvs, Unit4 and SYSPRO among others. According to AMR, "global ERP Software Market is expected to garner $41.69 billion by 2020, registering a CAGR of 7.2% during the forecast period 2014 - 2020." According to MarketWatch, the ERP Market Size is projected to be around US$ 49.0 billion by 2024.

The ERP systems appeared in the mid-1970s and the first incumbents (SAP, Baan, Oracle, JD Edwards, PeopleSoft and others) were established by the mid-1980s. These companies ruled the sector for several decades but since the beginning of this century several marked changes redefined both the business model and the competition scope. This industry can be divided into four phases.

**Phase 1**

Since the mid-1970s, a few iconic large ERP solution providers ruled this sector based on a business model capable of installing modularized packages for specific functional activities such as finance, purchase, sales, manufacturing and inventory control. In that period, customer relationship management (CRM) module solutions had a secondary role and were expected to deliver tools for email blasting, tracking of emails, prospecting, etc. During these 30 years, this industry faced a strong consolidation and in 2003 the leading incumbents were SAP and Oracle.

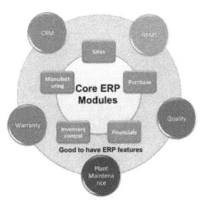

Figure 72 - ERP Modules in the early ages

**Phase 2**

During the mid-2000s, the incumbents began their movement towards creating open-innovation platforms, SAP Netweaver.

------------------

Suggested reading
*A Brief History of SAP NetWeaver* by Naren Chawla

------------------

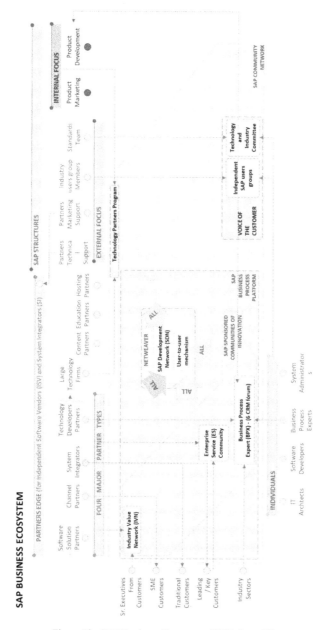

Figure 73 - SAP Business Ecosystem (ERP phase 02)

The creation of complex ecosystems with multiple subsystems combined community environments and sponsored closed innovation platforms. Later in 2009 Oracle announced the settlement of Open Innovation Centers in the US, in the UK, Japan and Turkey.

This second phase illustrates the incumbent's reaction to a changing business environment and their adaptation to deliver products and services at a faster pace, offering more variety and competing with the growing number of small specialized service providers.

**Phase 3**

Over the last decade, since the early 2010s, some capable service providers emerged showing the capacity to capture digital consumer behavior.

New icons, such as Salesforce.com, Amazon Web Services and Google Cloud – digital natives – positioned themselves as businesses capable of capturing demand signals from consumers by actively interacting – not only in the social media, but on the web.

These new players forced the beginning of commoditization of ERP legacy solutions based on installed modules and reduced the perceived strategic contribution given by traditional incumbents such as SAP and Oracle.

--------------

Suggested reading

**Legacy ERP**

- 5 Pitfalls of Legacy ERP Systems by Hector Bonilla
- 7 Ways Your Legacy ERP System is Holding You Back by Martin Davis
- How is Cloud Based ERP better than Legacy ERP?

--------------

Salesforce.com illustrates the type of solution that represents an asymmetric competitor to traditional ERP business incumbents.

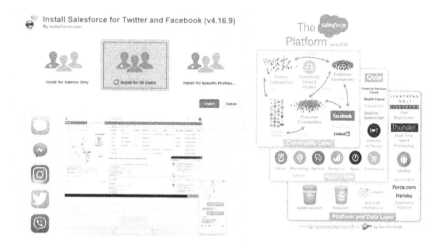

Figure 74 - Salesforce.com: digital native & social media integrated

While incumbents have received most corporate IT investments since the 1970s (Phases 1 and 2), now client organizations are allocating their financial resources to IT solutions that can capture digital consumer behavior, and therefore enhance sales.

Salesforce was born interfaced with Twitter, Facebook, LinkedIn, Instagram and other social media and offered the possibility of better understanding demand, plan sales and generate revenue to the industry (manufacturers and service providers).

These features were grouped and marketed as CRM solutions - now with very different features from those expected for CRM packages in Phase 1. This period had a severe impact on traditional incumbents, as illustrated in the following diagrams.

Oracle's <u>revenue flattened</u> since 2011:

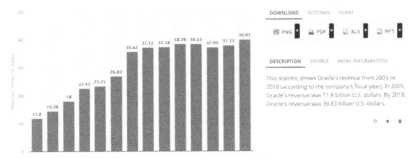

Figure 75 - Oracle's revenue since 2011

SAP and Oracle <u>market share are reducing</u> in the customer-related solutions:

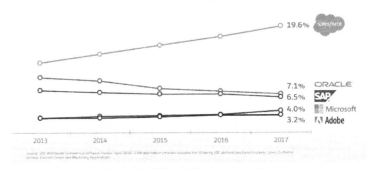

Figure 76 - SAP and Oracle market share

The transition began in 2010 with the growth of Salesforce.com, the decrease of Oracle and the stagnation of SAP:

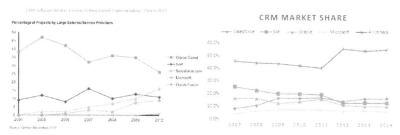

Figure 77 - CRM Market share

While the incumbent´s market share is shrinking, the overall market has grown fast:

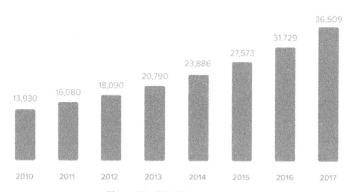

Figure 78 - CRM Market growth

Now, most new IT projects associated to data management as a strategic asset prioritizes CRM solutions, which can capture and give visibility of a real demand signal that is triggered in the digital world.

119

From the traditional incumbents' perspective (SAP and Oracle), they are now left to a secondary role – simply data storage, data base consulting and some level of sequencing when workflows are implemented.

Another player to watch at this stage and beyond would be Microsoft. Strength in the personal computing installed base and the increased share in the Point of Sales systems across the retail and payment interface systems in machine to machine payments makes it a credible contender to add more challenges to the incumbents.

Microsoft is also a significant player in the cloud business area. Rooting from a closed innovation environment, products such as Azure and Dynamics opened up the system to external parties to collaborate and innovate, effectively moderated and curated by Microsoft team.

The recent acquisitions of Microsoft in the Internet of Things business, as well as strategic alliances with companies such as NVIDIA, Intel and the established network of value-added retailer partners could give Microsoft the capability to challenge and make it even more difficult for Oracle and SAP to sustain their relevance.

Therefore, the third phase of the ERP industry suggests a new emerging business model, with new digital-native organizations gaining market share and reducing previous market leaders to a secondary role soon.

------------------

Suggested reading

- CRM forecasts and market estimates by Louis Columbus
- CRM Market Share Report by Chuck Schaeffer
- CRM - why is it important to your business? By Jennifer Lund
- Microsoft is set to pour $5 billion into the IoT by Nicholas Shields

------------------

**Phase 4**

More recently IBM announced the Open Power Foundation. A digital platform focused on group partners capable of developing hardware and software technologies to capture, transfer, process and analyze the increasing volume of demand signals generated in the web and interfaces with companies leading Phase 3 of the ERP industry (Salesforce, Amazon and Google).

----------------

Suggested reading and videos

- Open Power, Current Members
- The Value of OpenPOWER
- OpenPOWER, a catalyst for Open Innovation

------------------

In parallel, IBM developed its IBM Cloud Platform, IBM Watson IoT Platform and IBM Watson Data Platform, which resulted from closed innovation environments. Therefore, there is a clear strategy to combine the open innovation ecosystem with closed innovation strategies – as we saw in the late-2000s with SAP and Oracle.

This fourth phase is another pushback for the traditional ERP industry incumbents such as SAP and Oracle as the strategic solution for the organizations are now associated with how the digital demand signal is captured at the individual level (phase 3, Salesforce, Amazon, Google) and how they are processed (phase 4, IBM).

Although IBM and its initiative does not represent a competitor to ERP incumbents, it plays an important role in the business ecosystem and whatever strategy must balance the opportunity to partner with it.

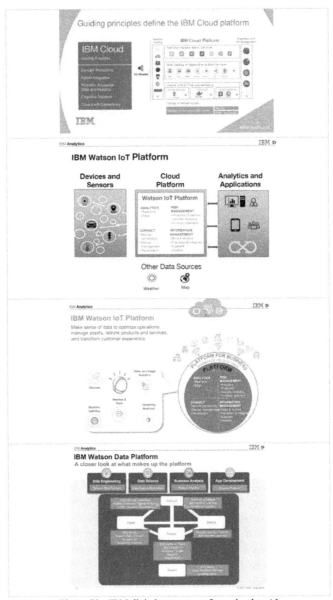

Figure 79 - IBM digital ecosystem: from cloud to AI

We illustrate this below using some images produced by IBM to communicate how they can interface the entire ERP ecosystem. The strengthening of players such as IBM becomes even clearer when the iconic organizations from phases 1, 2 and 3 rush to peer with them – as seen in these videos.

*Figure 80 - IBM: preferred partner (videos)*

## Building the digital ecosystem (SAP, Phase 2)

SAP built a complex environment that operates a multisided platform which I have named "SAP BUSINESS ECOSYSTEM" (SBE), illustrated in Figure 73.

--------------

Suggested reading

*A guide to the SAP Ecosystem, 2008*

--------------

Through SBE, SAP coordinates autonomous sub-systems that are orchestrated to balance the network effects produced in the SAP Community Network and the traditional activities with internal focus.

## How does SAP categorize different parties?

SAP uses multiple criteria to categorize the parties in its ecosystem. From my perspective, there are four relevant groups of stakeholders: customers, partners, individuals and SAP structures.

## The ERP Business overview

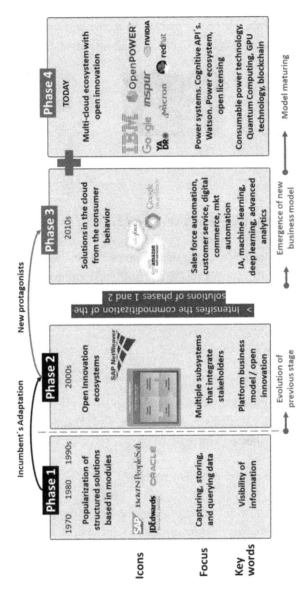

Figure 81 - ERP industry evolution: overview

**Customers**

SAP used a sales-channel criterion to identify two types of customers: traditional customers and small and medium enterprises (SME).

Simultaneously, from the product development perspective, SAP identified at least another three types of customers: senior executives (a niche across all customers); key customers; and preferred industry sectors.

These criteria (sales-channel and product development) are used simultaneously, therefore it is not possible to avoid the overlap between them. For example, within the traditional customers, some companies are considered key customers (such as Whirlpool). Senior executives are also associated to traditional customers. Moreover, the ten selected preferred industry sectors are populated by traditional customers.

The role of each customer type is explained in the answers for question 2 and 3, when the interaction with other parties of the business ecosystem is detailed.

Figure 82 – SAP customers' segmentation

**Partners**

This is the most complex group, with at least eight types identified (including subgroups). SAP structured the PartnerEdge Program to coordinate the efforts associated to multiple ISV (Independent Software Vendors) and SI (System Integrators).

The four major partner types are:

- the software solutions providers [Top 25 in 2017]
- channel partners [Best SAP CP, 2019]
- technology developers
- system integrators.

Some of these major partners joined a technology partners program for large technology firms. I have also identified three other types of partners: content, education; and hosting.

Figure 83 – SAP Partners

**SAP Structures**

I have identified both internal-focus structures (product marketing and product development) and external-focus structures.

Acting with focus on the Sap Community Network, there are four categories: partners technical support, partners marketing support, industry users' group and standard teams.

Figure 84 – SAP Structures

## Individuals

This group is populated by the community of professionals, not necessarily en-gaged as employees at SAP, its customers or its partners. They are software de-velopers, IT architects, business process experts, system administrators and sev-eral other technical activities.

This population is perceived as the "voice of the customer" in independent SAP users' communities [Where?], and in technology and industry committees.

Figure 85 – Individuals

SAP strategically promotes network effects in its SAP Community Network, more actively in the Business Process Platform. Interactions within members are carefully thought out and directed to specific ecosystems as I will explain in the following parts of this case.

## The multiple sides of the SAP platform

If we analyze each part involved in the SAP Business Ecosystem, they can be grouped according to six categories (highlighted in yellow in Figure 86), delimiting the six sides of the SAP complex platform business model. These are:

- three categories of customers (SME, traditional and leading);
- two types of partners (major and others);
- the individuals (expert community); and
- the SAP structures (internal-focused and external focused).

Traditional customers: SAP had (in 2009) more than 11,000 customers in its installed base. It has more than $200M in annual revenue. In the first moment, when SAP was designing and building its platform ecosystem, it expected to see broad adoption by partners before adopting the platform themselves.

Leading/Key customers: In the early stages, SAP worked closely with key trusted customers such as Whirlpool, Goodyear Dunlop and Zeiss to pioneer new composite applications in the Business Process Platform. Later, SAP built the Enterprise Service (ES) Community "by inviting leading customers and partners to work collaboratively to define the exact specification that would be used by internal SAP developers to create the next round of enhancements to the platform."

SME: These are small-to-medium-sized enterprises (SMEs) that have less than $200M in annual revenue and are supported by Channel partners that "provided industry and business-specific expertise to SMEs for cost effective and timely deployment of SAP solutions".

Major partners: "SAP actively managed four major partner types to rapidly expand and enhance the engagement with ISVs:

1) System Integrators;

2) channel partners;

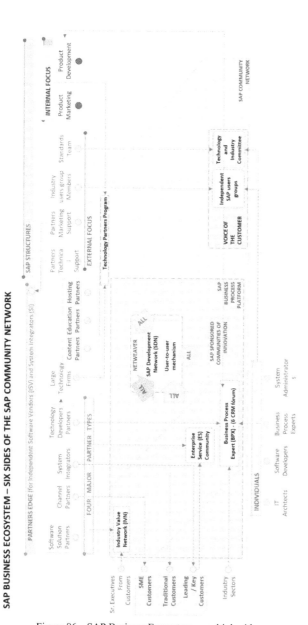

Figure 86 – SAP Business Ecosystem – multiple sides

3) technology partners; and

4) software partners".

Other partners: "Other partner categories included content partners, education partners, hosting partners, etc."

Individuals (expert community): IT people (such as software developers, IT architects, and system administrators) that interact in independent SAP User groups/communities in various countries and are actively engaged in a variety of technology and industry standards communities

SAP external-focus: SAP teams directly involved in the SAP Community network and in supporting its stakeholders such as partners, customers or independent community members. These teams include technical and marketing support, members in industry user groups and the standards team.

SAP internal-focus: SAP resources dedicated to the basics of product marketing, management and development. This structure accounts for the revenue driven by new software licenses sold to customers.

**Potential conflicts**

---------------

Suggested reading

- Governance in Multi-sided Platforms by J. Mattila and T. Seppälä
- Digital Platforms regulation by P.Nooren, N.Gorp, N.Eijk & R. Fathaigh
- Platforms, Open/User Innovation by E. Altman and M. Tushman
- Regulating 'Platform Power' by Orla Lynskey
- Digital Platforms by A.Asadullah, I.Faik & A.Kankanhalli

---------------

I have identified 17 points for potential conflict in the SAP Business Ecosystem:.

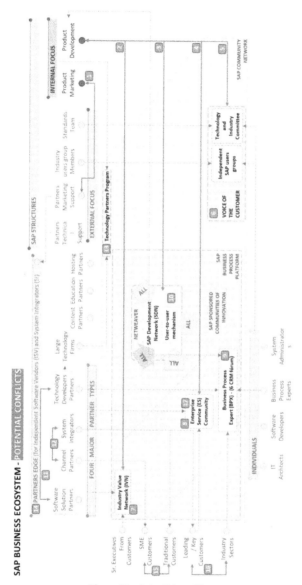

Figure 87 – Potential conflicts

## Resolving the conflicts

Major partners: There are several mitigation mechanisms identified for the major partners. This is expected as they are the strategy platform side that peers with SAP customers.

| Potential Conflicts (PC) | Risks' Mitigation mechanisms (text excerpts) |
|---|---|
| **PC#14: within major partners** > the main risk is that these partners do not have enough incentive mechanisms to keep investing in: | (1) Product-development incentives: SAP provides specific solution maps that outlines, over three years horizon, the areas of IT functionality and categorizes as "completely covered" to "elementary covered" to "not covered" by SAP's applications. This give direction to its major partners about its development strategy; Clear opportunities are left with a white space open for partner solutions; - SAP encourages the creation of diverse offerings from our partners, ensures and certifies that customers find and use them. |
| - time in the relationships with SAP and customers and; <br><br> - money in the new developments | (2) Marketing incentives: "Powered by NetWeaver" partners can use the SAP brand logo to demonstrate to customers their proven interoperability with SAP solutions, and they were listed in the SAP partner catalog; The marketing support with different levels of engagements depending on how well the partner solutions complemented SAP's own offering; SAP may organize joint analyst events or offer partners a forum at SAP's customer events; - SAP may agree to act as a reseller for the partner. |

SAP Figure 88 - Potential conflicts - SAP (a)

Internal structures: There are conflicts associated to the movement that "require a mindset shift within the SAP organization" and some internal structures may feel uncomfortable with such change.

| otential Conflicts (PC) | Risks' Mitigation mechanisms (text excerpts) |
|---|---|
| **PC#01: within marketing teams >** The marketing-team with internal focus and the marketing team that supports the partners (specially Tier 2 and Tier 1) need to dispute for the share of attention and resources | Info not available.<br><br>Suggestion: To have a clear influence of each structure's performance success (internal and external) on the other's performance evaluation could promote a more effective collaborative environment. |
| **PC#02: internal product development team (IPDT) and IVN** (Industry Value Network) > Ecosystem used by SAP to look ahead and assess the shape of future industrial change and to potentially influence its direction and trajectory. This external structure reduces the influence of internal product development team. | Info not available.<br><br>Suggestion: To have a clear influence of the IVN structure performance success on IPDT's performance evaluation could promote a more effective collaborative environment. |
| **PC#03: Internal product development team and SDN** (SAP Development Network) > When the question "whether SAP would build something themselves or would partner or would buy", this reduces the organizational influence of internal product development team that may have to do only support activities such as organizing product information, for taking a product to market. | According to the text, SAP still devotes significant attention and resources to the basics of product management and development as a significant portion of revenue is driven by new software licenses sold to customers. |

| otential Conflicts (PC) | Risks' Mitigation mechanisms (text excerpts) |
|---|---|
| **PC#04: Internal product development team and ES** (Enterprise Service Community) > When SAP invites leading customers and selected partners to collaboratively develop core services to be provided in its platform and to define the exact specification to be used by internal SAP developers, it reduces the influence of these internal structures | SAP focused on 10 functions or industries see business case, exhibit 5, which enables internal product team to have *a priori* visibility of the developments and organize their resources to keep properly engaged. |
| **PC#17: SAP legal team and ES** (Enterprise Service Community) > When SAP invites leading customers and selected partners to collaboratively develop core services to be provided in its platform this raises issues related to clear rights to the intellectual property (IP), patents and licenses of the products | To prevent this scenario, participation in the ES community was based on a legal agreement that established a clear IP framework. |
| **PC#05: internal product development team and "communities"** > The working relationships with independent SAP User groups/communities in various countries, to ensure customer feedback was incorporated into product development. This is an additional control mechanism over internal product development team that used to have more independency. The communities-enabled co-innovation reduces the influence of the internal product development team. | SAP orchestrates the communities so that peer-to-peer connectivity takes place across all SAP stakeholders.<br><br>SAP also created a Standards team that actively engaged in a variety of technology and industry standards communities, shaping standards to maintain an SAP advantage and/or create a level playing field for all vendors. |

Figure 89 - Potential conflicts - SAP (b)

Subsystems: Some of the conflicts are associated to the interaction with customers or even within the customer

| Potential Conflicts (PC) | Risks' Mitigation mechanisms (text excerpts) |
|---|---|
| **PC#06: within "voice of the customer" communities** > Once the standard teams join communities, they are exposed to public customer feedback, which can be either positive or negative. Additionally, the work of the standard teams in the technology and industry committees may expose SAP's strategic directions different from market trends or expectations. | Info not available.<br><br>Suggestion: To have a clear governance mechanism to identify, capture and communicate any market sensitive information to senior positions within SAP. The role of SAP people in these communities are not only technical, but also institutional. |
| **PC#07: within IVN** (Industry Value network) > There are three types of potential conflicts within IVN: (1) the presence of sr. executives with position in competing firms, (2) the competition within the selected SAP partners as different ISV may offer similar solutions and (3) between SAP and partners that have not been selected to join IVN. | Info not available.<br><br>Suggestion: To have a clear selection criterion to invite partners for each initiative within IVN, to not invite more than one competing Independent Software Vendor to join each initiative and to have transparent communication on the product development and applications within the senior executives. |
| **PC#08: within ES** (Enterprise Service Community) > There are two types of potential conflicts within ES: (1) the presence of competing customers and (2) the competition within SAP partners as different ISV may offer similar solutions. | |
| **PC#09: within BPX** (Business Process Expert) > By enabling collaboration types such as "SAP customer-to-SAP response", "customer-to-customer", "customer-to-partner" via discussion in six different CRM forums with a diversity of customers, users, partners, analysts with different backgrounds. | Parts interact with SAP product management, as there are moderators in all six CRM forums that come from SAP product management organization. Forum moderation work as "an integral part of what product management is supposed to be". |

| Potential Conflicts (PC) | Risks' Mitigation mechanisms (text excerpts) |
|---|---|
| **PC#10: within SDN** (SAP Development Network) > Wholesale rethinking on behalf of SAP towards its potential partners to encourage the creation of diverse offerings from our partners, ensure and certify that they work on our systems, and create ways for our customers to find and use them. Quality? | SAP setup a structured partner program called SAP PartnerEdge to manage partners and provide enablement services, certifications, and basic support services to partners. The creation of a certification program (Powered by NetWeaver) that ensured the high-quality technical integration of third-party software with SAP NetWeaver. |
| **PC#11: Software Solution Partners vs. Technology Developers Partners** > Potential conflict between SAP and partners not selected to join as TDP. | SAP setup a structured partner program called SAP PartnerEdge to manage partners and provide enablement services, certifications, and basic support services to partners. |
| **PC#12: Channel Partners vs. System Integrators** > there is a potential overlap between channel partners, system integrators and other ISV in the definition of a customer as being SME or not. The rule of $200M in annual revenue may not be easily audited. | Info not available. <br><br> Suggestion: Publicize each customer's P&L (Profit & Loss Account). There should not be a problem for a $1,000M business or a $50M; but grey areas may occur around $ 200M. |
| **PC#13: Large Technology Firms (LTF)** > Potential conflict within LTF as the initiatives with SAP may have concurrent development scope or applications. | Info not available. <br><br> Suggestion: To have a clear governance mechanism publicize the scope of each initiative within LTF and share with them. |

Figure 90 - Potential conflicts - SAP (c)

Customers: Some of the conflicts are associated to the interaction with customers or even within customers.

| Potential Conflicts (PC) | Risks' Mitigation mechanisms (text excerpts) |
|---|---|
| **PC#15: SME Customers vs Traditional Customers** > potential conflicts between SAP and traditional customers (+11,000 companies) due to the fear SAP is redirecting attention and resources to support SME customers. | Channel partners were developed to specifically target solutions to enterprises that had less than $200M in annual revenue. Channel partners provided industry and business-specific expertise to SMEs for cost effective and timely deployment of SAP solutions. |
| **PC#16: Leading / Key Customers vs. Industry Sectors** > Key/leading customers that do not belong with the ten sectors selected by SAP to be addressed in the SAP Enterprises Services (ES) Community. | Other communities such as IVN (Industry Value Network), BPX (Business Process Expert) and the Technology Partners Program offer solid ecosystems to nest eventual leading customers that are not part of the 10 selected industries for the ES. |

Figure 91 - Potential conflicts - SAP (d)

**Systems of engagement**

SAP began its journey with NetWeaver – "an interoperable internet-based Application Platform that is fully compatible with third party platforms and other SAP components and applications". It is used for various SAP Business Suites and receives a great deal of industry attention.

To leverage its platform model, SAP started to work closely with key customers and soon compiled a list of over 1,500 customers who had implemented at least one application solution on the Business Process platform. This early one-sided access strategy attracted the second side of the platform: the partners.

The envisioned business model had the following features and expectations:

137

- To engage customers, partners, and the SAP internal organizations with each other
- Peer-to-peer connection enabled by SAP technology and business process understanding
- The connection had to be between organizations and the individuals within those organizations
- It needed both formal and informal ties in the ecosystem
- To build communities and attract partners
- Accessing the knowledge outside of its own borders was critical to both customer and partner effectiveness
- To enable the various members of SAP's ecosystem to interact with each other
- To enable customers to view enterprise IT as a core asset that enabled adaptation and innovation for the long term;

**Does SAP have an effective system of engagement for its ecosystem partners?**

I have previously presented the conflicts according to the type of stakeholder: major partners, SAP internal structures, conflicts within subsystems (platform such as BPX and IVN) and conflicts within customers.

According to that analysis, it is clear that SAP has a strong system of engagement with multiple categories of incentives to their platforms stakeholders. Although some potential conflicts are not clearly addressed in the business case (which does not necessarily mean they do not exist), the most critical points – related to the major partners, SME and the traditional customers – are effectively addressed by SAP conflict mitigation structures.

Therefore, yes, I believe SAP does have an effective system of engagement for its ecosystem partners.

These major partners and customers populate the strategic sub-systems in SAP Business Process Platform, such as **IVN** (Value Industry Network), **ES**

138

(Enterprise Service Community) and **BPX** (Business Process Expert) [01]. These sub-systems (digital platforms with specific purpose) enable network effect within these major partners, customers and individuals from the SAP community.

Additionally, together with the broad SAP community, the major partners populate the Netweaver-based SDN (SAP Development Network).

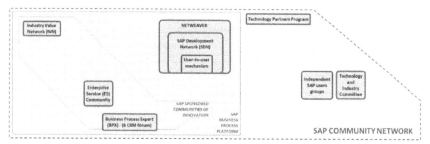

Figure 92 – SAP systems of engagement

SAP fosters engagement and participation by combining value proposition and the mechanisms of engagement. These are offered and executed through the elements of SAP Community Network.

| Platform structure | Value proposition | System of engagement |
|---|---|---|
| SAP Business Process Platform | Allows for the composition of new user-based services<br><br>Seamlessly leverages SAP's core applications and the fast-evolving web-based technologies<br><br>Enables customers with cost reductions in the short term and enables adaptation and innovation for the long term<br><br>Engages customers, partners, and the SAP internal organizations, including direct peer-to-peer connection<br><br>Access the knowledge that is outside SAP borders<br><br>Reaches out to ISVs to encourage the creation of new functionality on top of the SAP platform | Building and managing communities<br><br>Attracting partners with product and marketing incentives |

Figure 93 – Details of SAP systems of engagement (1)

| Platform structure | Value proposition | System of engagement |
|---|---|---|
| NetWeaver | Integration of business databases and processes from varied sources; First web-based cross-application, fully interoperable platform that can be used for developing SAP and others' applications; | Exploits web services technologies from Microsoft, Sun and IBM; Fully compatible with third party platforms; Boosts a common runtime environment; Allows for the composition of new user-based enterprise services that seamlessly leveraged SAP's core applications and the fast-evolving web-based technologies |
| SAP Developer Network SDN | Increases the productivity of IT people; User-to-user support mechanism; Allows co-innovation among its members; | The learning and collaboration that happens in SDN supports the productivity User-to-user support mechanism reduced calls to SAP staff |

Figure 94 – Details of SAP systems of engagement (2)

| Platform structure | Value proposition | System of engagement |
|---|---|---|
| Business Process Expert (BPX) community | Connects ecosystem members responsible for creating models of new ways for enterprises to connect internally and externally Enables collaboration in change management, project leadership, and industry best practices | Community members define new interaction models and business processes that challenges existing technologies and implementation; Allows for the sharing of industry-specific solution maps and interactions within process experts and tech developers, to assess feasibility of new processes. Interaction within members and with SAP product moderators in all six CRM forums that come from SAP product management organization. Forum moderation works as "an integral part of what product management is supposed to be" |

| Platform structure | Value proposition | System of engagement |
|---|---|---|
| Enterprise Services (ES) Community | "Value added" that SAP provided on its platform can be specific to either a business function (e.g., procurement, supply chain management) or industry (e.g., banking, energy, public sector). | Selected partners invited by SAP to join in (membership on an invitation)<br><br>Invites **leading customers** and **partners** to work collaboratively to define the exact specification that would be used by **internal SAP developers** to create the next round of enhancements to the platform<br><br>Participation in the ES community was based on a legal agreement that established a clear IP framework. |

Figure 95 – Details of SAP systems of engagement (3)

| Platform structure | Value proposition | System of engagement |
|---|---|---|
| Industry Value Networks (IVN | Looks ahead and assesses the shape of future industrial change and to potentially influence its direction and trajectory. | |

Figure 96 – Details of SAP systems of engagement (4)

| Platform structure | Value proposition | System of engagement |
|---|---|---|
| Standards team | Shaping standards to maintain an SAP advantage and/or create a level playing field for all vendors | Engages in a variety of technology and industry standards communities and shapes standards to maintain an advantage or create a level playing field. |
| Working relationships | Ensure customer feedback is incorporated into product development; keep an open, healthy dialogue with customers on wide variety of topics. | Guarantees working relationships |

| Platform structure | Value proposition | System of engagement |
|---|---|---|
| Technology Partner Program | The Technology Partners Program was established to build strategic relationships between SAP and other large technology firms such as Adobe, Intel, and Microsoft that could result in joint technology development mutually benefitting all parties. | |

Figure 97 – Details of SAP systems of engagement (5)

# Educational Sector Case Study

## 7. University: new digital strategy

I selected to analyze the University of Campinas (UNICAMP), where I hold a BA in Chemical Engineering and where I am currently a PhD candidate. I also concluded an MBA in Finance (2008) at UNICAMP and have lectured on Supply Chain Management (2004-2007) and more recently on Data Science Strategies. I have a comprehensive understanding of the institution built up during the last 25 years.

UNICAMP was listed $2^{nd}$ in Latin America and $33^{rd}$ in the world according to the Times Higher Education (THE) Emerging Economies University Rankings 2018. Brazil retains its status as the third most-represented nation, following China ($1^{st}$) and India ($2^{nd}$).

> *"This ranking includes only institutions in countries classified by the FTSE as "advanced emerging", "secondary emerging" or "frontier".*
>
> *- Advanced emerging: Brazil, Czech Republic, Greece, Hungary, Malaysia, Mexico, Poland, South Africa, Taiwan, Thailand, Turkey;*
>
> *- Secondary emerging: Chile, China, Colombia, Egypt, India, Indonesia, Pakistan, Peru, Philippines, Qatar, Russian Federation, UAE;*
>
> *- Frontier: 28 countries;*

*The rank uses the same 13 performance indicators as the World University Rankings to judge institutions on their teaching, research, knowledge transfer and international outlook. However, they are recalibrated to reflect the development priorities of universities in emerging economies."*

**The performance indicators are grouped into five areas:**

- Teaching (the learning environment); 30%
- Research (volume, income and reputation); 30%
- Citations (research influence); 20%
- International outlook (staff, students and research); 10%
- Industry income (knowledge transfer). 10%

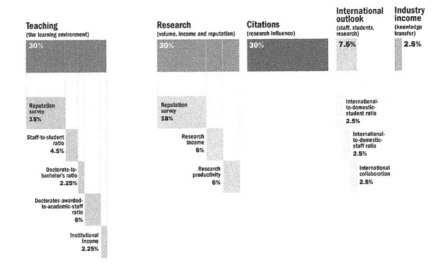

Figure 98 – Educational performance indicators

According to its own website, UNICAMP also claims to be:

- Top Brazilian university in number of published articles per faculty member.
- Responsible for ~8% of Brazil's articles in scientific journals.
- 46% of our graduate courses are top grades (ranked by CAPES/MEC).
- Top Brazilian university in number of patents.
- 15th: world's top 50 universities under 50 years old.
- 2nd: Latin America's top 10 universities (QS Ranking)
- 9th: top BRIC's universities.

144

Today, 99% of its faculty (1,759) have a Doctorate diploma. There are 18,338 students in the 70 undergraduate academic programs that were awarded 2,249 types of diplomas. There are 16,195 graduate students in 156 graduate programs (master's– 74; doctorate – 68 and specialization – 14).

## Segmenting the customers

### Traditional segmentation

According to UNICAMP's Statistics Year document, students that joined the university in 2017 are categorized according to the following criteria: time spent in private/public schools; type of previous education (standard/technical); family average income (4 levels); and race. This is the typical existing approach to understand the profile of its students.

Angulo presented in his article in entitled "A market segmentation approach for higher education based on rational and emotional factors", published in the Journal of Marketing for Higher Education, a thorough literature review of the traditional segmentation for undergraduate students and captured both rational and emotional perspectives of students and universities:

| Perspective | Focus | Underlining Factor |
|---|---|---|
| Rational | University | Academic and career opportunities; Quality and high standard; Image; Infrastructure and physical facilities; Cost and tuition fees; Scholarship |
| | | Selectivity |
| | | Distance from home |
| | Individual | Duration of search / process |
| | | Self-efficacy, vocational interest, choice goals |
| Emotional | Individual | Sociocultural influence (family, friends; barriers and supports) |
| | | Intrinsic (identity construction; personal values, wishes, and expectations; psychological; relaxation and leisure) |
| | University | Romantic or exotic quality to the sights, sounds, and smells of traditional institutions |

Figure 99 – Traditional customer segmentation

145

**New segmentation**

The challenge in this case is to identify the best categorization capable of offering the adequate value proposition to future undergraduate students.

In his work, Angulo explored the integration of "rational and emotional factors in higher education segmentation, following a call for a broader framework that could better account for the diversity of attributes that prospective students' value in their selection of a university". He proposed the following structure with four groups of features:

- 14 rational attributes related to the question "How important are the following attributes of a university to be chosen?"
- 11 emotional attributes related to the question "Why are you going to study at university?"
- 11 emotional goals related to the question "How do you see yourself in six years/when you finish university?"

**Sociodemographic information**

The results, which identified 6 types of customers that combine the listed features, is presented and adapted in the following figure:

| Segment/ Cluster | Rational Factors | Emotional Factors | Emotional Goals |
|---|---|---|---|
| 1. The independent | Strategic alliances Image | Independent Be able to manage on one's own Enjoy oneself | Self-confident |
| 2. The entrepreneur | Strategic alliances Academic and career opportunities | Enhance economic status and welfare | Entrepreneur Focused on self-development |
| 3. The rational | Quality and high standard | Be a great professional Improve quality of life | |
| 4. The dreamer | Image quality and high standard cost | Long for improving oneself Least focused on being able to manage on one's own | |

| Segment/ Cluster | Rational Factors | Emotional Factors | Emotional Goals |
|---|---|---|---|
| 5. The hard worker | Infrastructure and physical facilities/ cost | Improve economic welfare Achieve personal goals | Professional |
| 6. The emotional | Infrastructure and physical facilities Academic and career opportunities Image | Help parents out Achieve personal goals | Recognized |

Figure 100 – New customer segmentation

## Marketing alternatives

In another study, entitled "Student Target Marketing Strategies for Universities", the authors suggested an approach called "behavioral segmentation scheme", with two dimensions of attributes:

(1) The benefits sought by the consumer; and

(2) the underlying motivations of that consumption.

## There are three types of educational buyers:

1. Quality buyer: A student who demands high-quality services and is not overly concerned with costs. He or she wants the best and is willing and able to pay.

2. Value buyer: A student who demands good value as defined by a fair quality-to-price ratio. He or she looks for high quality for the money spent and expects service levels to match price levels.

3. Economy buyer: A student primarily interested in minimizing financial, as well as acquisition costs and tends to favor the least expensive and most easily purchased service offering. He or she is a consumer willing to accept marginal quality if the price is right and the acquisition is convenient.

147

**There are four motivational types of learners:**

1. Career learner: A student whose primary motivation for seeking educational services is career-oriented. This individual seeks specific skills and preparation that will enhance chances for successful job entry, advancement, mobility, and security, as well as improve chances for increased compensation, career satisfaction and social class advancement.

2. Socio-improvement learner: A student whose primary motive for seeking educational services is to improve the mind, broaden horizons, expand general knowledge, realize potential, do his or her own thing, and achieve other personal goals. Self-actualization is the major need that motivates this educational consumer.

3. Leisure-learner: A student whose primary motive for seeking educational services is the entertainment and/or recreational value provided by those services. These individuals desire educational services that provide enjoyable learning experiences, allows escapism, permits socialization, enhances quality of life, broadens knowledge of subjects of personal interest and promotes general mental welfare.

4. Ambivalent learner: A student learner whose primary motive for seeking educational services is other-directed, unknown or unclear. This individual seeks educational services in order to satisfy someone else (perhaps parents), to identify possible interests, to gain direction, or to avoid other life experiences.

The resulting matrix illustrates a variation for the concepts presented in Figure 101. Therefore, the six types of customers presented by Angulo well accommodates these 12 combinations of features well. This approach also guarantees there is not too much targeting.

The contribution from this work strongly relies on how to address these types of customers. The authors suggest three target marketing alternatives:

1) differentiated marketing;

2) concentrated marketing; or

3) orchestrated marketing.

| Types of educational buyers | Motivational types of learners | | | |
|---|---|---|---|---|
| | Career learner | Socio-improve-ment learner | Leisure-learner | Ambiva-lent learner |
| Quality buyer | 1 | 2 | 3 | 4 |
| Value buyer | 5 | 6 | 7 | 8 |
| Economy buyer | 9 | 10 | 11 | 12 |

Figure 101 - Motivational types of learners

------------

Suggested reading

• Differentiated Marketing vs. Concentrated Marketing by Chris Newton

• 5 Examples of Differentiated Marketing by John Spacey

• Concentrated Marketing by Hitesh Bhasin

• Marketing Orchestration

------------

Differentiated marketing involves the decision to operate in two or more segments of the market. A university might decide to select a limited number of clustered or scattered target markets. When this is done, the university has decided to pursue a "selected differentiated marketing approach." On the other hand, strategists at a university may elect to target each market segment, thereby following a "complete differentiated marketing approach." In either case, a distinct marketing program will be required for each individual market segment.

A high degree of focused effort characterizes concentrated marketing. This strategy takes one of two forms: "exclusive concentrated marketing" or "integrative concentrated marketing".

In exclusive concentrated marketing, a university focuses all the attention on a single segment of the educational consumer market in the hope of dominating that market through total market penetration. Integrative concentrated marketing is simply an extension of the exclusive strategy. This approach involves expanding a single market segment to encompass other similar segments.

Employment of integrative concentrated marketing entails using a developed exclusive market segment as a staging area for expansion into contiguous segments.

Market knowledge and marketing experiences gained in serving the original market segment enhance the chances for successful expansion. The strategy of orchestrated marketing consists of developing a selective marketing program designed to meet the common needs of a range ("horizontal" or "vertical") of market segments.

While the individual needs of each segment within a market segment range may vary somewhat, the orchestrated marketer finds a key commonality, basic characteristic or persuasive need that several otherwise different groups share.

Vertical orchestration focuses on the common clusters, aggregating different features together, while horizontal orchestration focuses on specific features across different clusters.

### Combining type of customers and marketing strategy

I opted to combine both modes and produce a new matrix. This is a decision framework to help select the comprehensive approach, considering the different types of customers. The next step is to define the value proposition for each segment/cluster.

| Segment/ Cluster | Differentiated Marketing | | Concentrated marketing | | Orchestrated marketing | |
|---|---|---|---|---|---|---|
| | Selected | Com-pletely | Exclusive | Integra-tive | Vertical | Horizontal |
| 1. The independent | | | | | | |
| 2. The entrepreneur | | | | | | |
| 3. The ra-tional | | | | | | |
| 4.        The dreamer | | | | | | |
| 5. The hard worker | | | | | | |
| 6. The emotional | | | | | | |

Figure 102 - Customer &marketing strategies

## Communication and value proposition

I have identified four types of content communication to be addressed to the six types of customers:

| Segment/ Cluster | Description (according to the author) | Type of communication that fits with the expected value proposition |
|---|---|---|
| 1. The independent | Individuals are independent and self-confident, looking for a university with a good image. | A) Strengthen the communication related to all sorts of rankings. |
| 2. The entrepreneur | Composed of students with a strong entrepreneurial intention, predomi-nantly male. | B) Strengthen communication of initiatives such as Unicamp Innovation Agency. |
| 3. The rational | Individuals seeking a high-quality standard and looking for a professional career. Emotional factors that matter to them are related to the material well-being, improved quality of life and professionalism. | C) Provide visibility of the suc-cess of its alumni, in different professions. |

151

| Segment/ Cluster | Description (according to the author) | Type of communication that fits with the expected value proposition |
|---|---|---|
| 4. The dreamer | Looks for image and high quality, but at low cost. Lack of fit between their aspirations and the reality. Tends to pursue a university career because he or she longs for personal development but at the same time is less focused on being able to manage on one's own. | D) Use the communication related to quality ranks and its alumni success but combine it with the visibility of:<br><br>- social protection programs designated to low-class students; |
| 5. The hard worker | Represents the hard working (majority female) students striving to improve their welfare and achieve their professional goals. | - opportunities for academic career within graduate courses |
| 6. The emotional | Comprises highly emotional students, attending public, low-cost schools, looking for recognition in their community and wishing to help their parents economically and achieve personal goals. | |

Figure 103 - Value proposition – communication

| Segment/ Cluster | Differentiated | | Concentrated | | Orchestrated | |
|---|---|---|---|---|---|---|
| | Selected | Completely | Exclusive | Integrative | Vertical | Horizontal |
| 1. The independent | | A | | | | |
| 2. The entrepreneur | | B | | | | |
| 3. The rational | | C | | | | |
| 4. The dreamer | | | | | | |
| 5. The hard worker | | | | | | D |
| 6. The emotional | | | | | | |

Figure 104 - Prioritization

## Customized Strategy Approach

The sequence, summarized in Figure 97, indicates the need to address four content market strategies. As we have been presented during the course videos, the Customize Strategy is about:

- Personalizing experiences based on customer behavior; and

- Making your offering adaptable to the different needs of customers

As a consequence, an effective personalization creates greater confidence in the relevance of the product. In this specific case of UNICAMP, the key metrics is associated to high scores in the selection exams which indicates the best students in the country have been attracted to the university.

According to Prof. Rogers, a variety of approaches to creating a customized experience for the customers are available: 1. Personalizing the commerce experience for a customer; 2. Personalized packaging; 3. Mixing and Matching Products; 4. Through targeted communications; and 5. Targeting on Customer Lifetime Value.

The Mixing and Matching Products strategy will be used to address the type of students categorized as "The dreamer", "The hard worker" and "The emotional" – associated to the horizontal orchestrated strategy.

The aggregated features are the search for low cost educational solutions, the need to improve their welfare and the need for community recognition.

Through targeted communications, Unicamp will address "The Independent", who look for a university with a good image. The goal is to strengthen the communication related to all sorts of rankings. "The entrepreneur" group will also receive targeted communications – focused on initiatives associated to innovation and launching startups. These are illustrated as "A" and "C" (completely marketing differentiated strategy) in Figure 103.

Finally, by targeting the student's lifetime value, strengthening the life-long success of its alumni, Unicamp will address "The rational" group.

**Marketing automation**

To automate marketing content delivery, Unicamp could create a website for high school students in which a preliminary form will capture the information related to the features illustrated in Figure 103.

153

-------------

Suggested reading

- The Ultimate Guide to Marketing Automation by Clodagh O'Brien
- Marketing Automation Strategy will need an AI-bot by Ankit Prakash
- What is marketing automation?

-------------

Based on that, Unicamp can understand in which behavioral segment each high school student belongs to and effectively interact with them during the three years prior to university entrance.

In the long run, as machine learning algorithms cross the historical data regarding customer profile and sent content, it will be possible to evaluate if the best-scoring students are those who received customized marketing content. Therefore, it will be possible to measure the response and continuously optimize the model.

**Customizing strategy – key challenges**

To close the loop, I double-checked the governance features and assessed if the key challenges associated to the Customizing Strategy were well addressed in the overall suggested strategy.

| Key challenges for Customize Strategy | Description (according to the author) |
|---|---|
| Customizing products/services affordably | The communication strategy is simple and requires little investment. |
| Giving customers confidence to choose | The goal is to communicate accordingly to each student's perception of value; therefore, it is expected to give them confidence to choose Unicamp as their first graduate school |
| Understanding which choices your customers care most about | The communication strategy is built from customers preferences, as explained in sections 3.1 and 3.2 |

| Key challenges for Customize Strategy | Description (according to the author) |
|---|---|
| Identifying motivations to personalize | The communication strategy is built from customers preferences, as explained in sections 3.1 and 3.2 |
| Getting the data | Explained in marketing automation |
| Using the data | Explained in marketing automation |
| Not being creepy | As mentioned in section 2.2a, the approach also guarantees there is not too much targeting. |

Figure 105 - Key challenges

# Dictionary Case Study

## 8. Digital consumer: collaborative behavior

In one of my areas of expertise, corporate governance, there are some online dictionaries that were prepared a few decades ago. They usually have around 200 words – most of them defined many years ago.

As in many other areas of knowledge, corporate governance is integrated to the business environment and exposed to new interactions. For example, there is a wide range of new words being used as the result of digital transformation such as asymmetric competition and digital disruption.

Unfortunately, the speed at which corporate governance dictionaries are updated does not deliver to the community the required quality. Therefore, I suggest a collaborative strategy to keep these dictionaries updated.

----------------

Suggested reading and video

**Multi-Sided Digital Platforms**

- Harvard Business School | Multi-Sided Platforms

- Uber, Airbnb, and ZoomThru By Richard Malone

- What's behind the success of multi-sided platforms?

----------------

**The collaboration mechanism**

I planned a three-sided digital platform with

(a) the community of corporate governance professionals

(b) the judges of the platform and

(c) the moderators.

The moderators are the platform owners, responsible for the ecosystem governance (once "bottom is not enough"). The online dictionary will start with the
traditional 200 words and expressions and a group of invited judges. There are
four key steps:

1. Contribution from the community

2. Judges' analysis

3. Judges' feedback

4. Moderator's decision

Figure 106 – Collaboration mechanism

Once the platform-based dictionary is open to the community, anyone can contribute to it by:

- suggesting additional explanation to existing words;

- offering definition for new words;

- requesting new words to be part of the dictionary.

The judges will evaluate the input that arrived from a community member with
either a positive or negative signal. This contribution will be accepted when 10
judges have assigned positive signals. The contribution will be refused if there
are three negative signals.

The moderatos will analyze each new approved word and have power to cancel it or recommend eventual adjustments. All rejected words (3 negative signals) are analyzed by the moderators, that may review the judges' decision.

**Governance rules**

----------------

Suggested reading and video

- Why you need a good model for digital governance by Howard Tiersky
- Data Governance for Platforms by S. Lee, L. Zhu and R. Jeffery
- Digital platforms are governing systems by David Sutcliffe
- Governing Bad Behavior in Multi-Sided Platforms by D. Evans

----------------

Several governance rules will be in place and monitored by the platform moderator to assure that:

- Judges that give positive signals to approved words are rewarded
- Judges that give negative signals to disapproved words are rewarded
- Community members that contribute are rewarded

To promote a truly reward-based mechanisms, according to accumulated score, some judges may be categorized as **"experienced"** while the community members with higher scores are categorized as **"silver"** or **"gold"** contributors. Community members may be invited to join as judge while judges may be downsized to community members.

**Motivation, modularity and skill level**

The proposed mechanism promotes active collaboration through "solving the existing gap", "open competition" and "open platform". It also has a structure that allows modularity and recognizes and rewards different skill levels.

158

- **Solving the expertise gap**: the contribution from the community (4) and the judges (1) will guarantee fast and precise update of the dictionary, which strengthens its relevance.

| | | Motivation | | | | | |
|---|---|---|---|---|---|---|---|
| | | Judges | | | Community | | |
| | Active collaboration | Love | Glory | Money | Love | Glory | Money |
| Approaches | Solving the expertise gap | 1 | | | 4 | | |
| | Crowdfunding | | | | | | |
| | Open competition | 2 | | | 5 | | |
| | Open platform | 3 | | | 6 | | |
| | Skill level | 7 | | | 8 | | |
| | Modularity | 9 | | | | | |

Figure 107 – Collaboration motivation

- **Open competition**: the judges compete (2) to provide both fast and accurate evaluation for the contribution from the community. The higher the score, more recognition – as they may become an "experienced judge". Similar effect occurs with the community members (6), that may become "silver" or "gold" members – or even be invited to join as a judge.

- **Open platform**: the model is a three-sided open platform (3), as previously explained.

- **Skill level**: once any community member may contribute with any word or expression relevant to the community, it may occur by suggesting from simple to very complex definitions. Therefore, the open platform model is accessible to (7) most members. The key governance element is the high-skill-level judges (8) who evaluate the contribution from the community.

- **Modularity**: In fact, this is a highly modular business model as each word/expression is a single unit.

## Co-authoring recognition

Any member of the community may generate a PDF version of the dictionary, which will recognize the contribution from judges and the communities by listing the names of experienced judges, judges, gold members, members and community members that contributes with at least one work/expression. For each confirmed contribution, the community member will receive a digital certificate that can be shared in the social medias.

--------------

Suggested reading

- Collaboration and Co-Creation by Gaurav Bhalla
- Collaboration and Co-Authoring in Word Online
- Crowd Authoring by Abdul Al Lily
- Co-Writing, Peer Editing, and Publishing in the Cloud by J. Dougherty

--------------

There are several benefits:

- Updated and complete document for the community
- Recognition within the community
- Contribution associated to an intrinsic belief in the cause
- Chance for fame
- Chance to be valued by peers

# GE Case Study

## 9. Brand equity: the GE case

### Background

This section was written based on excerpts from four articles.

- Learn Something New Every Day
- GE launches online news hub
- On Winning With Content + Keeping Score
- 5 Reasons GE's Content Goes Viral on Reddit

The aim of this section is to outline the value proposition expected from GE Reports initiative.

> *"GE Reports is an editorial-style hub that allows readers to subscribe and aggregate content they are interested in across GE healthcare, aviation, transport, energy, etc. It works across so many industries and issues with stories to many diverse audiences.*
>
> *GE Reports is a platform for those stories to be shared broadly across new media channels and GE expect to link this activity to wider industry conversations across multiple platforms. It packs up the work GE is doing and the industry insights they are able to provide into digestible pieces of compelling and relevant content. This content is primarily driven by trends, events and reader interest in technology, innovation and local impact.*
>
> *GE Reports is not a corporate website, it is a separate space where we can post news that responds directly to our audience's interests, just like a news site. Readers are encouraged to contribute and share their own stories and opinions and engage directly with the content via social media platforms.*

*Since 2008 the publication has evolved from a blog to a diverse magazine that serves a varied diet including the future of energy and healthcare as well as techno and "steampunk" photo essays. GE noticed the growth of credibility and audience as the magazine became a go-to place for lead communicators and marketers in GE's core industrial businesses in the US and abroad. GE Reports is now considered one of the best global corporate magazines. Its content resonates with a broad audience stretching from investors to geeks and technology enthusiast.*

*A key part of the puzzle is figuring out distribution. It's not enough to just come up with great stories, you must get the story out - you need to build an audience that will take it, engage with it, and share it through their networks. Quality is the first principle if brands want their content marketing to succeed as getting people to talk about and share that content is just as critical. Some stories were widely shared and picked up by other publications and all traffic linked back to GE Reports."*

## The value proposition

---------

Suggested reading

Useful Value Proposition Examples by Peep Laja

---------

The information presented illustrates how GE Reports is managed to contribute to build GE's brand equity. The success to deliver this value proposition is confirmed by the various prizes it has been awarded:

- Best Content Marketing of 2015 - Contently

- The 10 best content marketing efforts from 2015;

- 10 Best Big Company Blogs in the World - Schaefer Marketing Solutions

   *"...I'm happy to report that this stylish news magazine is on top again with exceptional story-telling that makes me go down the rabbit hole every time I visit the site. GE is trying to tell the world it has moved beyond appliances and if you love in-depth tech and science reporting, this is a great place to geek out and get lost. It doesn't feature its writers, which is a shame because there is such good work here."*

162

- Top 10 Brand Editors of 2014 - Contently

GE Reports named Best Blog: "*The standard fare for the average corporate blog usually consists of some companywide announcements, a profile of an executive or two, possibly some photos of a new project or a well-groomed campus. Rarely are they hubs for big-picture looks at the technological landscape or places where events are put in historical perspective.*

*That's what makes GE Reports, General Electric's daily blog, so appealing.... For the depth of its content, as well as its creative use of video, infographics, and slideshows, GE Reports is the winner of the Best Blog category of the 2013 PR Daily Awards.*

*The blog has garnered considerable attention, from publications including Wired, Fast Company, The New York Times, and Scientific American, as well as the blogs Gizmodo, TechCrunch, Mashable, and The Verge. The average visitor remained on the site for about a minute and a half, well above the typical amount of time Americans spend on websites.*"

Therefore, it is important to observe the success of GR Reports from the brand equity perspective. I have selected some of the metrics that seemed to be more appropriate to GE and classified them into audience, channel-based engagement, universal engagement, and financial metrics.

**Selected metrics**

Audience

"*According to GE Report Editor-in-Chief Tomas Kellner, GE laments the difficulty of measuring "the totality of audience", although they use a combination of Google Analytics, Quantcast, and GoSquared to track key metrics like visitors, time spent, and bounce rates. They are still looking for a metric that combines performance goals (page views, time spent, etc.) with media goals, like click-throughs and cost-per-click.*" (see articles cited in Background)

"*The blog has hundreds of thousands of devoted readers, its stories regularly go viral on Reddit and in the press, and coverage of it ultimately ties back to the GE*

163

*brand. GE illustrates an example when a GE Reports reader posted the story to Reddit, where it was quickly upvoted by the site's community and it soon made it to the top of the front page of the internet. Over a million people read the story."* (*see articles cited in Background*)

I suggest the following frequency metrics for Audience: number of unique readers for each article; number of unique readers for each business unit (aviation, energy, healthcare, etc.); number of unique readers per focus country; number of unique readers per category (innovation, perspectives, performance); combination of the results found for "frequencies" 1 to 4 above;

Channel engagement

*"GE Reports isn't just a website - it's a storage room and GE uses these assets like a Lego block that you can break up and use on different channels. Periscope, Snapchat, Facebook Live. GE has been one of the first brands on most social platforms, including Instagram, Periscope, and Snapchat."* (*see articles cited in Background*)

I suggest the following metrics for Channel Engagement:

- Number of stories shared broadly across new media channels

- Number of media channels that replicated GE Reports' stories

- Number of stories effectively linked through the mix of social, digital, broadcast and written content

- Number of stories shared by readers - Readers are encouraged to contribute and share their own stories and opinions and engage directly with the content via social media platforms

- Frequency of stories published per week - GE Reports publishes up to 10 stories a week

- Frequency of stories published in other GE Reports satellite sites – GE Reports has 15 other sites publishing content in Chinese, Japanese,

French and Russian and its content resonates with a broad audience stretching from investors to geeks and technology enthusiast

- Social Shares and Followers - track their social follower growth against their total number of shares.

"Marketers often get enamored by the latter, but the more valuable metric is an increase in social audience. These are opting in to future content from your brand. If both are increasing, this indicates that your organic social shares are reaching the right audience – and building it among those new people."

Share of Voice – "it measures how much your brand or product is talked about compared to your competitors for a specific topic. you can also use social trackers to measure the volume of conversation around your brand versus your competitors". In the case of GE Reports, it can be applied either to its categories, industries or selected countries. Other potential metrics that could be explored include repeat visitors, subscriptions, social likes and followers.

## Universal engagement

GE Reports links all stories through a mix of social, digital, broadcast and written content to build familiarity with business stakeholders and tell GE's story. (*see articles cited in Background*)

> "*For multi-location*, distributed brands, brand equity can also produce the following benefits: Drive purchase decisions / Build customer loyalty / Increase market share / Protect pricing decisions / Support global growth / Increase word-of-mouth referrals"

And this is the situation reflected in GE Reports as it is segmented by (a) categories, (b) industries and (c) countries.

I suggest the following metrics for Universal Engagement:

- Drive purchase decisions – monitor if big contract decision makers are GE Reports readers;

165

- Build customer loyalty – monitor is repeated clientes have GE report decision maker readers;

- Increase market share – monitor if new clients have GE report decision maker readers;

- Brand relevance: "The extent to which your customers agree your brand provides unique and specific value that is not offered by your competitors." ref.53

Some methodologies include surveys and focus groups; web traffic or search volume for GE brand and products; and social mentions and reviews

### Aided recall / unaided recall of the brand

*"Three ways to determine how your assets for local marketers are translating into output are:  Local marketer campaign and asset utilization / Sales on promoted products / Customer adoption of loyalty programs."*

With "Local Marketing Automation", brand managers can also conduct A/B testing between similar markets to compare output and subsequent results. That can be done for categories, business units or countries.

--------------

Suggested reading

- Compare 16 local marketing automation platforms
- What is Local Marketing Automation?

--------------

### Financial metrics

John Wanamaker´s quote "Half the money I spend on advertising is wasted. The trouble is, I don't know which half." It really applies to GE Reports' mixed and multi-layer strategy. As presented before in this case:

166

*"It uses these assets like a Lego block that you can break up and use on different channels. Periscope, Snapchat, Facebook."*

*"It links all stories through a mix of social, digital, broadcast and written content to build familiarity with business stakeholders and tell GE's story."*

I suggest the following metrics for Financials:

- Market share: *"The percentage of overall sales in your industry that your market takes in; The metric quantifies the brands share of the market and can be divided into customer segments, product segments and geographical markets. It is an indication of the brands ability to retain and more importantly, attract new customers"*

- To connect this metric to GE Reports it is important to register (a) if the decision makers in their customers are reader of the news hub and (b) if these decision makes feel they were somehow influenced by the content they usually have access to. This effect is called "engagement loyalty" and can be evaluated with surveys and interviews.

The capacity to evaluate the engagement loyalty impact is also important when measuring the following metrics:

- Transaction value: The price customer will pay GE´s product or service for. It is likely that GE´s brand equity plays a role in the pricing strategy, now positively influenced by GE Reports.

- Price premium: GE's ability to offer its product or service for a higher-than-average price to increase its appeal. Again, it is likely that GE´s brand equity plays a role in the pricing strategy, now positively influenced by GE Reports.

- Revenue generation and potential: The amount of money GE makes by selling products or services, and the potential revenue to be made if trends continue.

- Other potential metrics include price premium over competition, average transaction value, customer lifetime value and rate of sustained growth

------------

### Suggested reading

- Content Marketing ROI by Shafqat Islam
- Why brand equity is important & how to measure it by Alicia Honeycutt
- Brand Equity Models and Measurement
- Leveraging Brand Assets for Killer Local Marketing Campaigns
- Branding By The Numbers

------------

# Freight Transport Case Study

## 10. Freight transport: not yet a success

**Freight Transport Overview**

The Brazilian cargo freight transport sector represents approximately 2.5% of the GDP. Brazil has the fourth largest road network in the world with 1.75 million kilometers (preceded by the USA, India and China). The Brazilian Transport Ministry estimates nearly 2.7 million vehicles are operating nationwide, most of them for more than 5 years, nearly 38% of these vehicles are conducted by low educated self-employed drivers. Finally, due to geographic and demographic patterns, trucks are empty in nearly 40% of the kilometers they complete.

The challenge to match the need to move forward industry production and the available trucks and drivers looking for their next journey, has long attracted the attention of companies offering digital solutions. The promise is to create value by reducing trucks´ idle time (including routes without cargo) and by reducing overall cycle time as product owners find the adequate truck type faster for its product.

In 2012, Visa launched a freight-match service focusing on truck drivers who were looking for return freights from regions where shipping activities were scarce. Product owners registered their products on Visa´s website and the truck drivers accessed the information in kiosks at petrol stations. Visa intended to gain driver's loyalty and expand cardholder's basis. The initiative did not scale up and was soon discontinued, mostly because of the limited number of kiosks and erratic actions to promote it within the drivers' community.

Figure 108 - Visa Prepaid Card for Truck Drivers (Brazil, 2012)

Since 2015, new business models have become stronger as several digital platforms are connecting drivers to goods. These platforms produce interaction through Hybrid Apps that are generally known as the "Uber for Trucks".

---

App

App is an abbreviated form of the word "application." An application is a software program that's designed to perform a specific function directly for the user or, in some cases, for another application program. Different types of apps include:

- Web app - stored on a remote server and delivered over the Internet through a browser interface.
- Native app - has been developed for use on a particular platform or device.
- Hybrid app - combines elements of both native and Web applications. Hybrid apps are often mentioned in the context of mobile computing.
- Killer app - a program that intentionally or unintentionally gets you to buy the system the application runs on.
- Legacy app - has been inherited from languages, platforms, and techniques earlier than current technology.

---

On the other hand, truck drivers usually have two or three of these apps and regularly check the best spot freight transport opportunity announced in each solution. From a driver's perspective, the apps selection criteria vary according to several attributes, including user experience on the platform. Issues related to price negotiation, product insurance and safety requirements are not moderated by these apps.

In fact, today we face a daily dispute involving at least six players ("P01", "P02", "P03", "P04", "P05" and "P06"). They are allegedly digital platforms, but reality shows important conceptual gaps. Some have gone international while other decided to grow locally first. Some see the drivers as the key consumer of their platform services while others understand it is the industry (cargo owners) that are their key customers. All of them promise high value network interactions, but they are still in the learning curve. Although massive self-promotion activities suggest strong market penetration, the challenges are enormous.

---------------

Suggested reading

- Monetize Your Blog and Online Digital Social Platform by Pam Moore
- How to monetize your startup? 25 Monetization models by Yuri Shub
- Pros and Cons of Using a Content Monetization Platform

---------------

**The Players**

P01 (QueroFrete) is supported by two startup accelerators: Wow (private) and Startup Brasil (public). The driver registers on the platform informing the vehicle type and characteristics, its capacity and geographical coverage. The firm that owns the cargo to be transported can use a filter option to select the trucks (and drivers) of their preference, before contacting them. Owners and drivers communicate through a chat solution available on the app, negotiate the price and agree on payment conditions. They claim to have 100,000 truck drivers on the platform.

P02 (Sontracarga) was created in 2014 and claims to have 140,000 truck drivers registered. The value proposition is to find a truck compatible to the products awaiting to be transported. The app suggests drivers to product owners. The solution accepts four personas: self-employed driver, freight company, cargo agent (intermediary) and the industry (product owner). As other solutions, it offers a national coverage, it is integrated into Waze maps and is available for Google Chrome, Androids, iOS and Windows phone. The service is free to drivers and product owners.

P03 was established in 1988 as a website where freight announcements were posted. In 2000, the project was rebranded to "Fretenet" and expected to match products and drivers, but it did not gain scale and was discontinued in 2001. In 2006, they projected that a new start would be boosted by the exponential growth of the Internet, social medias and massification of smartphone use. New services were developed within the platform and in 2015, they were exclusively dedicated to a mobile channel. While the service is free for self-employed truck drivers, it charges a monthly fee from freight companies and from the industry. There is a paid option for some service providers, such as restaurants or resting locations, for them to be visible in the maps displayed in the App. Monetization occurs as suppliers of the community pay monthly fees. It claims to have more than 220,000 vehicles registered and to enables 81 million freight consultations every month. But when I checked, there were only 966 users online.

P04 (Buscacargas)claims to be a digital platform with a website and an app to facilitate the transportation of goods. The service is free for truck drivers who negotiate with cargo owners through a chat on the app. The filtering mechanism works for both sides: drivers can look for cargo announcements and the industry may search for specific types of trucks. P04 maintains the historic of transactions available for consultation. To enhance security experience, it allows cargo owners to access driver´s national ID and photos (of the driver and truck).

Although at first sight these solutions seem to be similar, a closer look shows each of them has a unique strategic value proposition, as seen in Figure 100. The discreet differences between them may be comparative or competitive advantages, depending on the personas their targeted community have.

| Platform | Value proposition | Resources | Intermediaries | Suppliers | Customers |
|---|---|---|---|---|---|
| P01 | Match product to be shipped and transport capacity (idle trucks) | Products (owners) Trucks (drivers*) | | Owners Drivers* | Owners Drivers* |
| P02 | Find truck driver to transport goods | Trucks (drivers*) | Cargo agent | Drivers* | Owners |
| P03 | Find products for self-employed truck drivers | Products (owners) | | Owners Freight companies | SE Drivers** |
| P04 | Help drivers to find goods and cargo owners to find the right truck | Products (owners) Trucks (drivers) | | Owners SE Drivers** | Owners SE Drivers** |
| P05 | Find truck driver to transport goods | Trucks (drivers*) | P05 (optional) | Drivers* | Owners |
| P06 | Find products for self-employed truck drivers | Products (owners) | | Owners Freight companies | SE Drivers*** |

Figure 109 - Six incumbents
* self-employed and freight companies (usually small businesses)
** SE, self-employed
*** SE, self-employed, but tend to accept freight companies soon

There are two other companies strongly disputing the market share within this community: P05 and P06. Apparently, these companies have captured the attention of investors around the globe and now play a game that combines the management of strategic alliances to enhance value through more significant network effects and the need to grow exponentially.

 P05 (CargoX) was founded in 2014 by a former CTO at UBER, Frederico Vega, and a former COO da Coyote Logistics, Eddie Leshin. At an early stage, Goldman Sachs invested approximately US$ 20 million. Other investors, such as George Soros, Qualcomm Ventures, Agility Logistics and Valor Capital Group added another US$ 14 million in investments. Despite international investments, and according to several announcements, in the short term they focus on expanding in the Brazilian market, leaving internationalization for a second moment. [Recent news]

In 2017, its revenue achieved US$ 50 million revenue, placing them among the top 20 freight businesses in Brazil. CB Insights listed CargoX as one of the 30 most disruptive startups in the world in 2018 (Game Changers list). This list has 22 companies in the USA and the others are in the UK, Russia, Canada, China, United Arab Emirates and Brazil.

P05 has 240 employees, 150,000 drivers and 250,000 vehicles registered, 1,000 customers (cargo owners) and announces to facilitate up to 600 journeys every day. It is a platform that aggregates pre-approved truck drivers and monitors their localization. When a customer (cargo owner) announces the need to transport a product, the platform searches for the driver that can execute the task more efficiently and sends him a request. This model shows a bias in favor of the cargo owner. P05 has a license to transport goods, and therefore it may provide cargo insurance and other transport documentation.

P05 claims to have a solid approach to treat big data and they have recently (Jan 2018) announced it now accepts bitcoins as a means of payment. It has recently announced the arrival of a digital media expert as company´s CTO. His focus is to intensify the technological changes imposed by the market to expand user experience for drivers and cargo owners in the platform.

"P06"

P06 (Truckpad) was launched in 2013, and soon after, it received an investment from Plug and Play, one of the world´s largest startup accelerators. They claim to have 700,00 drivers and 350,000 vehicles registered, more than 120,000 downloads of its App and 70,000 daily accesses from 50,000 self-employed drivers. The P05 digital community collaborates with developers such as Movile, Apontador and Maplink. They have received several prizes such as Startup Weekend, Lide Futuro and Endeavor Brasil.

The service is always paid for by the freight companies that hire the self-employed drivers either as a fixed value that varies up to US$ 1500.00 per month or as a percental of each operation, ranging from 2.5% to 5% of the agreed freight value.

The business model encourages self-employed drivers to download an app on their smartphones and register with very little initial information, such as vehicle characteristics. The driver accesses the transport opportunities posted on the app and may start negotiating directly with the product owner via a chat integrated into the App. At first, there is no need to unveil the driver´s telephone number or email. This model shows a bias in favor of the driver.

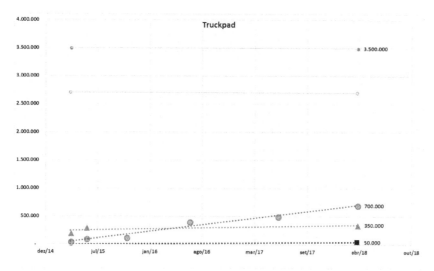

Figure 110 – P06 evolution

On the other hand, from the industry perspective, the platform searches within 600,000 registered drivers who are (now) within 50 km from the shipping point and that matches certain truck characteristics and may contact them. This model shows a bias in favor of the cargo owner and balances the platform experience.

Mercedes-Benz has recently bought a minor part of P06 participation and became the third shareholder of the company and expects the platform now to include freight companies – so far, only self-employee drivers are part of the community. The founder is the main shareholders (48%) and the tech group Movile comes second. One third of the registered vehicles in the platform are Mercedes. Another alliance was celebrated with Sascar, a vehicle tracking device producer

175

that use satellite technology. Drivers with Sascar's device installed have priority to be assigned to goods.

The long-term strategy is based on Market Intelligence initiatives based on the knowledge on drivers' behavior, such as the routes they drive through, their preferred resting locations, the number of working hours and, obviously, the type of truck they use.

There are two key areas to be developed: digital media, focusing on advertisements in the platform; and mobile commerce, with recommendation of products and services to truck drivers.

The goal is to create scalable solutions keeping the structure lean; today P05 has approximately 50 employees and operates in Brazil Argentina, Chile, Colombia, Mexico, Uruguay and Venezuela.

Although P06 has not yet achieved break-even point, this is said to be the result of the continuous and intensive platform development strategy. However, it seems that the growth rate is disappointing – in April 2018 they reported only 50,000 active users (less than 1.5% of the total market).

**The leading platforms**

When compared, it is possible to understand the two biggest digital cargo freight sector players have a specific approach, as illustrated in the next figure.

| Platform | Value proposition | Bias | International | Investments | Collaboration | Tech drivers |
|---|---|---|---|---|---|---|
| P05 | Find truck driver to transport goods | For the cargo owner | Not now | Goldman Sachs, George Soros, Qualcomm Ventures, Agility Logistics, Valor Capital Group | | Blockchain, Bitcoin. Big data analytics |

| P06 | Find products for self-employed truck drivers | Balanced | Already began | Plug and Play, Movile, Mercedes-Benz, Shell, Michelin | Apontador, Maplink, Sascar | Big Data analytics |
|---|---|---|---|---|---|---|

*Figure 111 - The leading platforms*

## The SWOT analysis

If we consider the sum of interactions produced by these six solutions, then we may delimitate the existing digital freight transport market in Brazil.

To simplify the analysis, I decided to focus on the network effect produced by P05 and P06, the leading platforms in terms of the number of members. This is a reasonable approach as from the users' perspective as these two platforms offer non-mutually exclusive services.

| | Platform | Value proposition | Resources | Intermediaries | Suppliers | Consumers |
|---|---|---|---|---|---|---|
| + | P05 | Find truck driver to transport goods | Trucks (drivers*) | P05 (optional) | Drivers* | Owners |
| | P06 | Find products for self-employed truck drivers | Products (owners) | | Owners, Freight companies | SE Drivers** |
| = | Simplified Brazilian Digital Freight Transport Market | (*A) Find truck driver to transport goods and find products for self-employed truck drivers | (*B) Trucks (drivers*) and products (owners) | (*C) Yes, it is possible | (*D) Drivers*, product owners and freight companies | (*E) product owners and truck drivers*** |

Figure 112 - Simplified freight market

\* self-employed and freight companies (usually small businesses)
\*\* SE, self-employed
\*\*\* SE, self-employed, but tend to accept freight companies in the near future

177

As a consequence of seeing the digital freight transport market in Brazil from this perspective, we can accept that:

1. The available platforms may add value to truck drivers and cargo owners

2. The platforms count on idle truck capacity and available products as resources for the community

3. The platforms may intermediate negotiation if members require it

5. The platforms have three *personas* as suppliers: drivers, offering transport capacity; product owners, offering goods to be transported; and freight companies, either offering idle transport capacity or good to be shipped

4. The available platforms may add value to truck drivers and cargo owners

6. The platforms count on idle truck capacity and available products as resources for the community

7. The platforms may intermediate negotiation if members require it

8. The platforms have two *personas* as consumers: drivers in need of goods to transport and product owners in need of vehicles

These characteristics illustrate the basics dynamics of the existing digital freight transport market in Brazil.

---------------------------

Digital Platforms - Key terms

Pipelines, Platforms, and the New Rules of Strategy

By Marshall Van Alstyne, Geoffrey G. Parker, Sangeet Choudary

1. Platform owners – have the rights over the brand and the intellectual property that define the ecosystem

2. Ecosystem – the totality of members from back office and Community subsystems, and the developers;

3. BackOffice – subsystem formed by the platform owners and the intermediaries; intermediaries are those participants who supply the means through which the solution is delivered, such as the smartphones used by the truck drivers

4. Community – subsystem formed by suppliers, consumers and its efforts to create value through interactions

5. Suppliers – participants that offer resources to the ecosystem

6. Resources are of two types - vehicles and goods

7. Consumers – those who use (need) the resources

8. Network – members of the community and the developers

9. Network effect – interaction that occurs within the community

10. Developers – members that create Solutions that promote high value network effect;

------------------------

**Identified strengths (S)**

S1. Digital technologies (DT) disintermediate the freight price negotiation between industry and self-employed truck drivers while the middle player, known as the cargo agent, usually captures up to 20% of each trip revenue.

**Identified weaknesses (W)**

W1. The speed drivers entering the platforms is very disappointing; the largest platform (P06) has 50,000 regular users, which is only 1.5% of the total number of vehicles – according to P06´s estimates (3.5 million vehicles). Other players surely have even lower penetration, not considering drivers that are counted as unique in different platforms. This evolution in 5 years (since 2013) is definitely worrying.

W2. The target members for these platforms are dispersed. Even though there is a higher concentration in the southeast region, where São Paulo and Rio de Janeiro are the biggest metropolitan regions, there is a variety of cities, truck sizes and types, different vehicle ages, high percentage of old vehicles that do not go through the Apps' selection filters, high percentage of old drivers who tend to be more resistant to new technologies, just to mention a few. (see T2)

**Identified opportunities (O)**

O1. To open the platforms to external service providers that can provide diversified user experience to drivers and product owners; there is no sign that the existing platforms are investing in creating environments that attract developers; as several management positions in these startups are occupied by executives grown in the traditional business, it seems they prefer to build walls to keep control rather than keep the doors open and then orchestrate the community members to enhance high value network interactions;

O2. Improve data availability; that involves the creation of mechanisms to motivate drivers to interact with the Apps, then collect and store data, and finally apply analytics routines to identify behavior patterns that can be used to attract members (drivers and service providers) that today are external to the platforms;

O3. Promote the creation of social groups to enhance interactivity within drivers; the social feeling shall increase retention and work as a magnet, attracting new drivers – therefore, new industry members;

**Identified threats (T)**

T1. If the driver perceives that the cargo agent adds value by offering high quality freight opportunities, the drivers may not completely migrate to use the disintermediated model proposed by the platform. (see S1)

T2. The platform owners must understand the market culture (W2) and lead a massive change management effort. However, this effort must occur on such a massive scale that it is not likely a few companies can do it;

**Consolidated perspective:**

| STRENGTHS | WEAKNESSES |
|---|---|
| S1. Digital technologies (DT) disintermediate the freight price negotiation between industry and self-employed truck drivers while the middle player known as the cargo agent usually receives up to 20% of each trip revenue. (see T1) | W1. The speed drivers entering the platforms is very disappointing; the largest platform (P05) has 50,000 regular users, which is less than 1.5% of the total number of vehicles – according to P05´s estimates (3,5 million vehicles). Other players surely have even lower penetration, not considering drivers that are counted as unique in different platforms. This evolution in 5 years (since 2013) is worrying.<br><br>W2. The target members for these platforms are dispersed. Even though there is a higher concentration in the southeast region, where São Paulo and Rio de Janeiro are the biggest metropolitan regions, there is a variety of cities, truck sizes and types, different vehicle ages, high percentage of old vehicles that do not go through the Apps' selection filters, high percentage of old drivers who tend to be more resistant to new technologies, just to mention a few. (see T2) |

Figure 113 - SWOT analysis (a)

| OPPORTUNITIES | THREATS |
|---|---|
| O1. To open the platforms to external service providers that can provide diversified user experience to drivers and product owners; there is no sign that the existing platforms are investing in creating environments that attract developers; as several management positions in these startups are occupied by executives grown in the traditional business, it seems they prefer to build walls to keep control rather than keep the doors open and then orchestrate the community members to enhance high value network interactions;<br><br>O2. Improve data availability; that involves creating mechanisms to motivate drivers to interact with the Apps, then collect and store data, and finally apply analytics routines to identify behavior patterns that can be used to attract members (drivers and service providers) that today are external to the platforms;<br><br>O3. Promote the creation of social groups to enhance interactivity within drivers; the social feeling shall increase retention | T1. If the drivers' perception that cargo agent adds value by offering high quality freight opportunities, the drivers may not completely migrate to use the disintermediated model proposed by the platform. (see S1)<br><br>T2. The platform owners must understand the market culture (W2) and lead a massive change management effort. However, this effort must occur on such a |

| and work as a magnet, attracting new drivers – therefore, new industry members; | massive scale that it is not likely a few companies can do it; |
|---|---|

Figure 114 - SWOT analysis (b)

## The SWOT analysis & the domains of digital transformation

*"Transforming a pre-digital business is a very different challenge than building a new start-up from scratch. These companies have a lot of strengths (existing customers, products, distribution, reputation), but they also have a lot of established habits, processes, and organizational culture rooted in their pre-digital years. For a traditional business to achieve its next stage of growth in the digital era, it needs to rethink its approach to strategy in five domains—customers, competition, data, innovation, and value."*

From: David Rogers: How Businesses Can Thrive In The Digital Age

**Customers:** The existing platforms sill see their customers – specially the truck drivers – as mass market and ignore the potential value generation that their interaction could create. Although the digital freight transport sector has been promoting, in a small scale, the disintermediation of the negotiation process between drivers and industry, it has not really modified the path to purchase. Apparently, the platforms have only digitally replicated the off-line experience.

------------------------------------

Websites that have a relevant value proposition to truckdrivers

- Transport topics
- Truckinginfo
- TruckingPlanet
- FleetOwner
- RoadKing
- TCI BCapital

------------------------------------

**Competition:** As suggested the existing digital platforms are not creating value by organizing an ecosystem of different parties. In fact, it there is tremendous bureaucracy for third parties to enter the communities. The effort to control, rather than harmonize drivers, industry and new entrants (such as developers and coopetitors) has restrained value creation within the community and, therefore, inhibited the expected growth. The slow market penetration rate is the most relevant threat to these platforms.

**Data:** The leading platforms are apparently mismanaging data. The general strategy is to increase the number of drivers with their Apps to collect geolocation data, which is treated as the ultimate asset – when it is not! The existing platform models are not incentivizing the growth of network interactions to produce diversified data. Nor are they trying to attract newcomers to their community to offer new services, produce new interactions and therefore, generate more quality data. The way data is being managed is a significant weakness of the digital freight transport sector.

**Innovation**: The leading platforms observed seem to be directed by "deciders in chief". The founders of P05 and P06 are supported by structures personal self-promoting image strategies that place them as the visionary leaders who had the great idea. Despite the fact they made the right move at the right time – which enabled their companies to lead this digital market at the moment, for the last several years their business seems to be directed to increasing the number of truck drivers in the community, but not necessarily creating relevant experience to them.

There are no signs that support the existence of rapid and constant experimentation; on the contrary, new initiatives are planned in the offices and are only announced when a comprehensive implementation plan is defined and ready to start. These businesses have not yet learned how to learn from their community. Nor have they understood that they should create value when the walls that impede the entrance of third parties are removed.

The need for a cultural change in the executive level and board level is a point to be evaluated carefully.

**Value:** The existing digital freight transport market in Brazil has not understood how to create value. Successful executives from the off-line traditional market are leading these platforms anchored in long-standing beliefs. The strategies in place are meant to capture existing superficial information and sell it via digital media. The lack of awareness that this mechanism produces a vicious cycle that in the long run will push drivers away, is a threat that cannot be underestimated.

------------

Suggested reading

The Problem with the "Uber for Trucking" Model

------------

# Airbnb Case Study

## 11. The (unhappy) customer journey

----------------

Suggested reading

**What are the digital touchpoints?**

- Digital Touchpoints – What Are They? by Greg Frye
- Digital Customer Touchpoints: Definition & Examples
- Understanding your Digital Touchpoints by Brian Sandiford
- The Many Digital Touchpoints of a Modern-Day Consumer
- Customer Touchpoints

----------------

**Previous experience**

In this assessment I report my fifth experience using Airbnb services. The previous experiences were in different cities:

- P1: I stayed in Rio de Janeiro (Brazil) with my wife for a couple of days;

- P2: I stayed in Granada (Spain) with my wife and two sons overnight;

- P3: I stayed in Sevilla (Spain) with my wife and two sons for three nights;

- P4: I stayed in Malaga (Spain) with my wife and two sons overnight;

The accumulative perception of Airbnb services was very positive and before my fifth experience I was advocating in favor of this platform. I frequently recommended it to friends, workmates and relatives.

To visualize how my involvement with the brand occurred, I defined a qualitative scale as seen in Figure 118. I defined a simple scale for the touchpoint experience intensity and considered that:

- 2 goods equals 1 very good;

- 3 goods makes 1 fantastic;

- 1 bad plus 1 very bad equals 1 terrible.

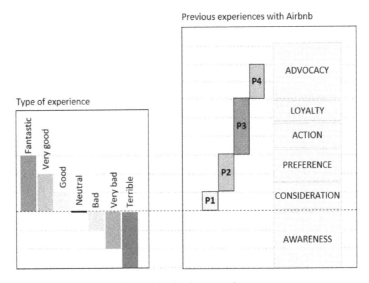

Figure 115 – Previous experience

**The path to purchase**

I structured my journey as a customer in seven moments that are detailed in this section. These phases cover the activities from an early search of options to post-use interactions with the brand. The goal was to go on vacation for nine days with my wife, my two sons, my mother and my father.

As we live in different cities, this is a unique opportunity for many parents to enjoy their grandsons. I had to observe that my mother has some mobility difficulty. I was looking for a house or a flat in a luxury location with a swimming pool and sports facilities. Ideally, a city close to my parents´ town (Rio de Janeiro, Brazil).

## Searching and evaluating the options

I started planning this vacation seven weeks in advance. I looked for some options at Booking.com narrowing the search based on date/period, city, type of room(s) and hotel category. I selected three options (B1, B2 and B3) that offered good price-location combinations.

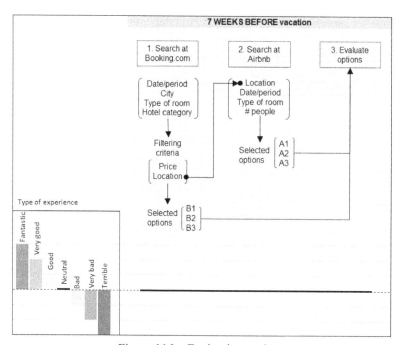

Figure 116 – Evaluating options

Then I visited the Airbnb website and searched for alternative options based on the locations I selected the hotels at Booking.com. I refined the search informing date/period, the type of room (house/flat) and the number of people in my group.

187

After evaluating some options, I selected another three possibilities (A1, A2 and A3).

Therefore, to this point I grouped six workable solutions: B1, B2, B3, A1, A2 and A3. I understand this process had a neutral impact in my user experience as it occurred exactly as I expected.

**Selecting the options**

I agreed with my wife on the priority list: B1 > A1 > A2 > B2 > A3 > B3. The first option was a hotel I found at Documenting.com but when I went back to the website the desired room was no longer available – that was a bad experience.

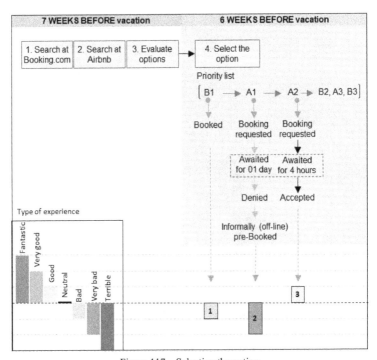

Figure 117 – Selecting the option

Then we moved to the second option (A1) at Airbnb. I selected the period I wanted and sent the request to the host, following the Airbnb procedures. The following day I received a message from the host informing that he had negotiated the house for someone else outside the platform – and the status at Airbnb was not updated. This was a very bad experience as I trusted the information available on the platform.

Finally, our request for the third option – second in Airbnb – was accepted within four hours. That was a good experience, especially when compared to the waiting time occurred in A1.

**Paperwork**

A few weeks after the agreement on where to stay, I had to upload copies of everyone's ID as part of the security control in the luxury building, we were going to.

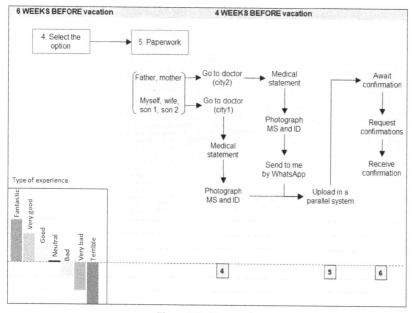

Figure 118 - Paperwork

Additionally, we all had to provide evidence of our good health condition to have access to the swimming pool – which required us all to go to a doctor. Although these rules were published by the host as policies for this flat, this uncomfortable offline user experience was a negative point in the process.

### The arrival day

When the host confirmed all the requested documentation was received, he gave the mobile number of his assistant. I had to send WhatsApp message four hours before arrival to be informed about the password to be used to unlock the apartment door.

I sent three messages but had no response. After I arrived at the destination, I called the host´s mobile who did not know the password. After some minutes, the host called me back and informed me of the password. We were all relieved to get into the apartment and be able to finally start our vacation.

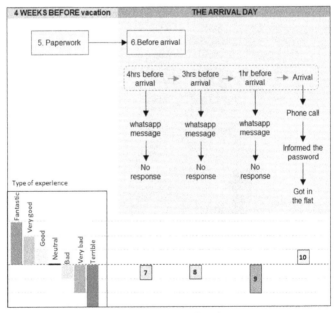

Figure 119 – The arrival day

## The vacation period

The opportunity to have the family together was a great experience, despite several minor issues related to the maintenance of the apartment, which were not expected in a "luxury" location.

The only significant problem was the water supply interruption on two different days. That occurred from 8am to 5pm due to unplanned maintenance in the building's pipeline.

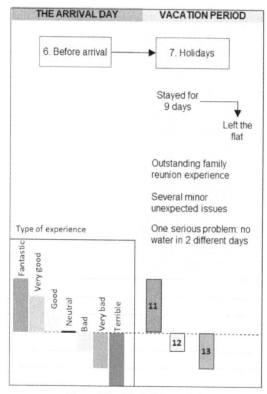

Figure 120 – The holiday period

## The week after

The worst part of my customer journey began in the day after we all left the flat.

The apartment owner sent me a message offering to refund 22% of the amount paid as long as I did not publish a testimonial of my experience on the Airbnb platform nor on any other online community. I had no idea of Airbnb's refund policy – I did not even know they had one. I was surprised by the host's offer and tried to negotiate. I offered my commitment to write a fair testimonial, listing the issues that happened and making his efforts clear to solve them as soon as possible – which really happened. However, he refused this agreement.

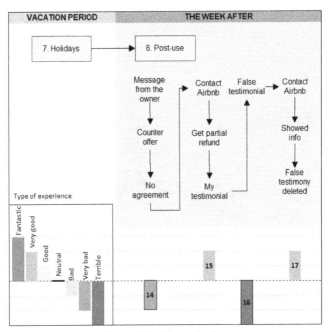

Figure 121 – The week after

Then I decided to contact Airbnb and I was informed that in cases of water supply interruption in the flat, the host had to refund the amount equivalent to the period without water. Therefore, two days out of nine makes 22! Based on the previous message sent by the host, which was posted on the Airbnb platform, the attendant understood the issue was confirmed and automatically processed my refund, without previous notice to the host.

After that, the host published a long testimonial with false statements. Once again, I contacted Airbnb, shared the content of all Whatsapp communications that proved his testimonial was false. The false testimonial was removed from the platform.

**The end of the user experience**

According to Airbnb´s policy, both the guest and host can publish testimonials about the event up to two weeks after the event is concluded.

Therefore, for another week after the false testimonial was deleted, I monitored the platform daily to check if any other false testimonial had been published. Fortunately, no other interaction happened. But that was definitely a very bad period.

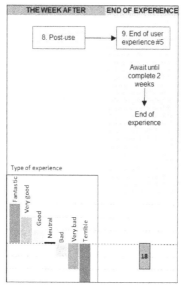

Figure 122 – The user experience

Although my final decision was the third option I selected, I was very confident as my previous experiences with Airbnb platform had been very positive. Figure 123 illustrates the process how I became close to the brand to the point of advocating for it. Unfortunately, this fifth experience had a negative overall evaluation, as seen in Figure 122. The sum of touchpoints experience resulted in a negative net perception.

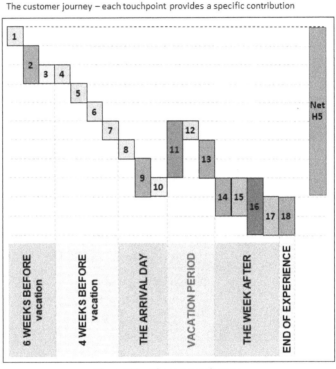

Figure 123 – The customer journey

**The touchpoints**

I believe it is important to group the touchpoints according to the type of interaction. When the touchpoints specifically related to the interface with Airbnb platform (Figure 123) the result is a positive perception. But when the experience

194

related to the touchpoints with the platform´s supplier (the host) are grouped, the ultimate experience is very negative.

This exposes the fragility and dependence of the platform´s brand on the quality of their suppliers. My future purchasing decisions will be highly influenced by the aggregate perception.

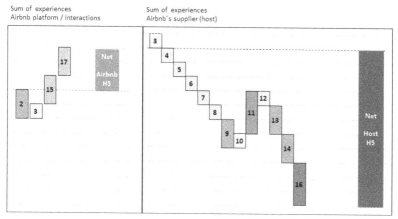

Figure 124 – The touchpoints

**Better experience**

Although I have achieved my ultimate specific goal of having an outstanding family reunion (touchpoint 11), the overall experience was very negative. The elements related to the quality of the supplier were determinant to create a frustrating perception of the platform´s brand. The touchpoints related to the supplier are the ones that could have offered a better experience.

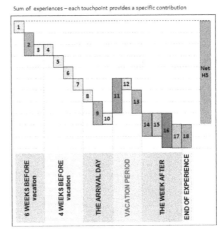

Figure 125 – Better experience

## Advocate for the brand

Give reasons to justify your response. For example, did you share or talk about it on any digital media platform? If so, how did you share your own experience and your decision with others in a way that might potentially influence them?

As explained, I was happy advocating for this brand before my fifth experience with them. But after this traumatic customer journey, I consider myself back to the awareness level. A practical consequence in that for my next vacation, which will be in 8 weeks´ time, I have not even considered using Airbnb. It may take a while until the relationship with this brand can be rebuilt.

To those friends, workmates and relatives I used to recommend Airbnb, I now share may recent experience and warn them to be very careful to seriously consider other options.

Today´s relationship with the brand

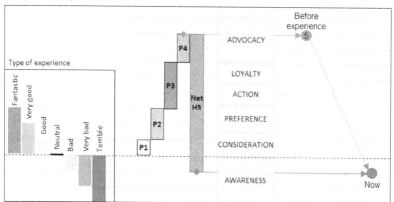

Figure 126 – Today

# Sony vs. iTunes Case Study

## 12. The music industry: Sony Music vs. iTunes

I have identified many groups of payers in the music industry. Each group shows specific dynamics when their member's role within the music industry is closely observed.

The first group is formed by the artists, including composers, lyricists, performing artists hired by record labels and independent artists. This is the only group the ORIGINATORS train.

The second group includes the record labels (Universal, Sony BMC, EMI and others), the independent producers, the mastering studios and the mixing engineers. This is the group that represents the PRODUCER train. The record labels partner with their hired performing artists for the royalties associated to the sound recording copyrights.

| | |
|---|---|
| 1 | Composers |
| 2 | Lyricists |
| 3 | Performing Artists |
| 4 | Independent Perf. Artists |
| 5 | Record Labels |
| 6 | Independent Producers |
| 7 | Mastering Studios |
| 8 | Mixing Engineers |
| 9 | Music Publishing Companies |
| 10 | MPC - Major |
| 11 | MPC - Major Affiliates |
| 12 | MPC - Independents |

Figure 127 – Music industry players

The third group are the MUSIC PUBLISHING COMPANIES (MPC), with three types of players: the majors (Sony, Warner and Universal), the major affiliates (or mini-majors: smaller publishing companies associated to the majors) and the independent publishing companies. The MPCs represent the composers and lyricists' interests associated to the musical composition copyright. Being primarily representants of originators' interests (composers – or songwriters - and lyricists), I assume MPC companies are also in the ORIGINATORS train.

-------------

Suggested reading

- What a Music Publishing Company Does by Heather Mcdonald
- How to Start Your Own Music Publishing Company by Jason Blume
- Music Publishers Directory
- Lyricist Vs. Songwriter

---------------

Therefore, although four players form the ARTISTS group, their members address their demand differently. While hired performing artists and record labels collaborate on one side, the composers, lyricists and MPC join forces on the other side. The independent artists will use independent producers or, eventually, try self-promoting initiatives.

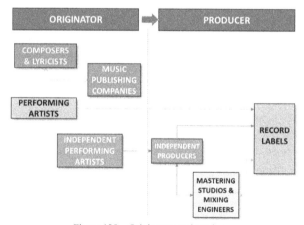

Figure 128 – Originators and producers

There are five different groups coexisting in the DISTRIBUTOR train:

- the traditional promotional channel members (radio, print, video, retail and public relations),
- the traditional sales structure members (distributor sales representative, retail chains, independent stores, writer publisher and the touring merchandizing),
- the digital distribution members (YouTube, Facebook and other social networks, internet radio, podcasts and blogs),
- non-interactive streaming online retail (Pandora, SiriusXM, AM/FM broadcasting stations) and
- interactive streaming online retail (Spotify, Apple Music, Google Play, iTunes).

--------------

Suggested reading

- What is digital distribution?
- What is a podcast?
- What is Non-Interactive Streaming?
- Interactive streaming by Kelsey Butterworth

--------------

To illustrate the intensity of correlations within all members of the music industry, I created the figure shown in Image 133. The color code indicates strong positive correlation (dark green), positive correlation (light green), relative indifference (grey), some conflict (light red) and strong conflict (dark red).

The area indicated as Model Transition represents the interaction of traditional music groups (Promotional Channels and Sales Structure) and recent digital groups (Digital Distributors, Interactive and Non-Interactive Online Retail).

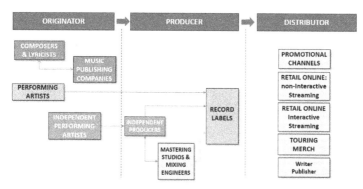

Figure 129 – Distributors

Although traditional structures have virtually disappeared, this matrix illustrates the existing members of the music industry. Given the goal of this case is to discuss specifically the roles of SONY and iTunes, I am not detailing the aspects of each interaction.

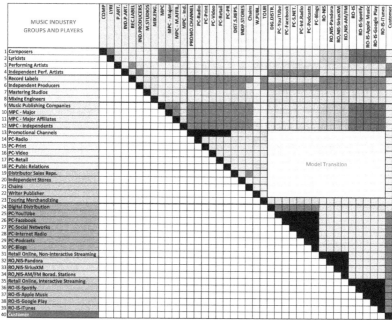

Figure 130 – Players' correlations

## Sony Corporation of America

While Sony/ATV Music Publishing LLC is an American music publishing company, Sony Music Entertainment is "a global recording music company with a roster of current artists that includes a broad array of both local artists and international superstars, as well as a vast catalog that comprises some of the most important recordings in history". Both companies are owned by Sony Corporation of America. Therefore, today SONY has roles in the PRODUCER train (as Record Label) and in the ORIGINATOR train (Music Publishing).

Figure 131 – Sony

According to Billboard, in 2017 recorded music generated US$4.03 billion (+14.9% vs. 2016); while music publishing Sony/ATV totaled US$ 670.5 million (+11.8%).

Back to digital, downloads fell to US$449 million (-16.1%), but overall when combining revenue from streaming and downloads, revenue grew 23.6%. Breaking out formats and product lines by percentage of total revenue, streaming accounted for 44.4%; physical for 30.2 %; downloads 11.2% and other 11.4%. [01]

The Orchard is another company wholly owned by Sony Music. It offers distribution services to independent artists and labels in various markets, including physical distribution to indie labels, but subsequently expanded the services they offer and started working with artists directly as well.

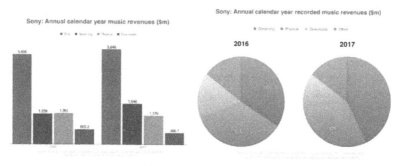

Figure 132 – SONY figures

Brad Navin, The Orchard CEO said "Our newly merged company is unique in structure, scale and reach. Coming together as one company that is both truly global and locally focused will allow us to take the service we provide to our artist and label partners to the next level.

The Orchard is the only global comprehensive digital and physical distribution platform with its own delivery, sales, distribution and reporting systems built specifically for independent clients. With a single deal, clients have the ability to deliver their music to every leading global and local digital and physical retailer and reach music fans around the world".

Figure 133 – The Orchard

With The Orchard, SONY assumes relevant roles in the DISTRIBUTOR train and strategically expands its influence on independent performance artists.

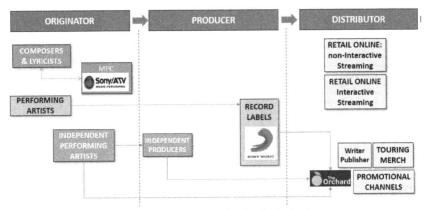

Figure 134 – The value train with The Orchard

## The distributor train

As introduced, in the DISTRIBUTOR train five different groups coexist. According to this case study's orientation, the focus is on iTunes (interactive streaming online retail group).

The business model for this group focuses on building direct relationships with the performing artists and selling the access service to the customer. According to Apple, iTunes is the best way to organize the music and movies you already have, in the same environment where you can buy the ones you still want. It allows uses (consumers) to stream over 45 million songs, ad-free. Or download albums and tracks to listen to offline.

The iTunes Store is available on all devices, which means you can buy that catchy song you just heard or rent that movie you've been meaning to see, anytime you want. And since your entire library of music and movies lives in iCloud, everything you buy is immediately available, no matter how you want to play it.

The iTunes, as well as Spotify, Apple Music, Google Music Play are interactive streaming online retail. According to HFA, interactive streaming is when a digital file is transmitted electronically to a computer or other device at the specific request of the end user in order to allow the end user to listen to a recording or a playlist contemporaneously with the user's request. Interactive streams are sometimes referred to as on-demand streams.

Streaming is already the main revenue segment in the American music industry.

Naturally, traditional Record Label companies resisted to this movement as they prefer to promote their own hired artists. When online retail offers interactive streaming with a huge amount of still unknown independent artists, and this platform gains scale, the Record Label companies – therefore their hired artists – lose money.

### MUSIC LABELS EMBRACE
### A RAPIDLY CHANGING BUSINESS

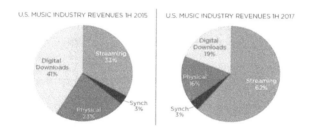

Figure 135 – Changing business

While in the previous traditional music industry, the customer only had access to those vinyl records from the artists that the Record Label decided to produce, now the options are incomparable.

Having eliminated the cost of physical distribution and reduced the cost of intermediaries, the final price for the consumer also reduced. Additionally, single tracks are available, and consumers do not need to pay for the complete album.
205

For a fixed price, and similar platforms offer unlimited access to any artist around the globe.

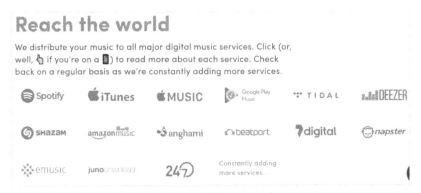

Figure 136 – Digital music service

Companies such as Record Union [digitally distribute any music - from artists located anywhere in the world - and make it available to both interactive and non-interactive streaming online retail services. It is important to notice that SONY´s The Orchard is offering this very same service!

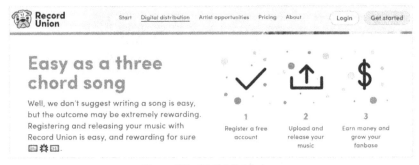

Figure 137 – Digital distributors

The Orchard business plays two roles in the DISTRIBUTOR train: as a channel distributor and as a channel promoter. As channel promoter, The Orchard may privilege efforts towards any online retail and influence which streaming service the consumer acquires.

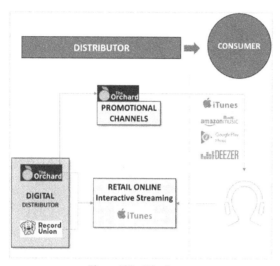

Figure 138 – Distributors

## SONY´s strategy

Four strategic movements SONY took after iTunes was launched in 2003 can be identified.

The first movement SONY made was towards the left value train extreme, reinforcing its relevance with the artistic class (composers, lyricists, hired performing artists and independent performing artists). This represents a wider approach compared to traditional behavior to represent only the hired artists (as any Record Label would do).

According to its website, "Sony/ATV Music Publishing is the world's No.1 music publishing company ... and now owns or administers more than 3 million copyrights .... It became a solely-owned Sony company in 2016. Since 2012

207

Sony/ATV has administered EMI Music Publishing, further extending the reach of the songs, songwriters and artists it represents. The company is a full-service music publisher with its interests including not only a world-class roster of songs and songwriters, but an industry-leading synchronization operation and production music businesses Extreme and EMI Production Music."

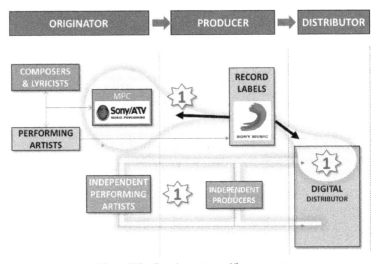

Figure 139 – Sony´s strategy – 1ˢᵗ movement

Sony/ATV represents artists' interests related to musical composition copyrights (composers and lyricists) and round recording copyrights (performing artists, mixing engineers, mastering studios and record labels).

--------------

Suggested reading

- Confused by Music Copyright? by Alexander K. Fleisher
- Breaking down copyrights in music by Justin M. Jacobson

----------------

During the second strategic movement, The Orchard was structured as a digital distributor for all artistic class (not only for SONY hired artists), including the

208

independent performers. With a global structure, The Orchard has the capacity to capture the products (music) from artists virtually anywhere.

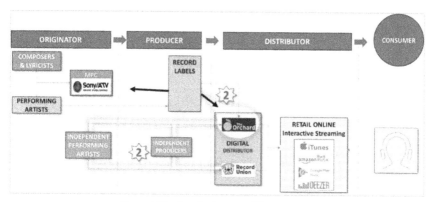

Figure 140 – Sony´s strategy – 2nd movement

According to its website, The Orchard "is the industry's leading independent distributor and label services company and comprises digital natives specialized in marketing, advertising, sync licensing, video monetization and performance rights services." Therefore, within the same corporate group (SONY Corporation of America), different companies execute similar services.

The third strategic movement used The Orchard again. SONY intensified its presence in the DISTRIBUTORS train by expanding its services to become a promotional channel.

In its website, The Orchard states that it "empowers artists and labels to connect with fans across the globe. From digital retailers and physical stores to performance rights societies and mobile outlets, our partnerships help amplifies your reach and revenue across multiple business verticals. The Orchard Workstation [01] offers robust content management, marketing and business intelligence tools to drive release strategy and provide real time insights."

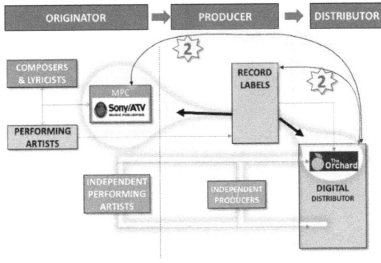

Figure 141 – Sony´s strategy – 3$^{rd}$ movement

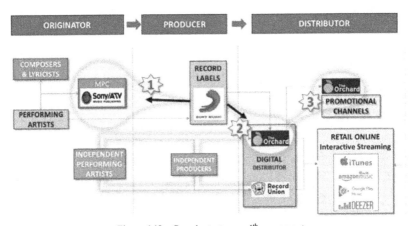

Figure 142 – Sony´s strategy – 4$^{th}$ movement

The last strategic movement is a discrete activity carried out by The Orchard as a promotional channel. It influences the consumer to acquire music from selected services.

210

Depending on the business interests of SONY, it may emphasize the acquisition of interactive or non-interactive ser-vices. Moreover, within these services, The Orchard may promote specific companies. For example, it may incentivize con-sumers to buy from Amazon Music instead of iTunes.

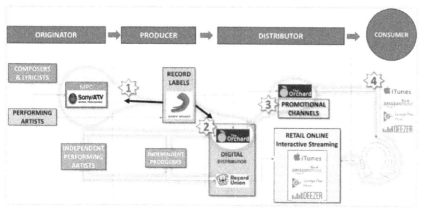

Figure 143 – Sony´s strategy – 5th movement

## Value and competition analysis

In this section, I address the specific questions proposed for the case. Some of these questions were explained in the previous sections while other requested additional comments. The firm I focused my analysis was Sony and its interaction with Apple´s iTunes.

## Value exchange

Arrows pointing to the right (value being delivered downstream):

- Arrow A: Artists, including composers and lyricists, producing the "raw materials"
- Arrow B: The record labels producing music on a large scale, from the "raw materials" provided by the originators
- Arrow C: The online retail companies making the tracks (and albums) available to the consumers;

Arrows pointing to the left (value delivered upstream – monetary, data, marketing support):

- Arrow D: Consumer paying the online retailers
- Arrow E: "Promotional Channels" offering marketing services to "Record Labels" and "Digital Distributor" offering distribution services to "Record Labels" (in these cases, SONY has companies for both ends of this arrow). "Online retailers" paying sound recording copyrights to "Record Labels", which transfers part of the value to their hired performing artists.
- Arrow F: "Online retailers" paying music composition copyrights to "Music Publishing Companies", which transfers part of the value to their hired composers and lyricists.

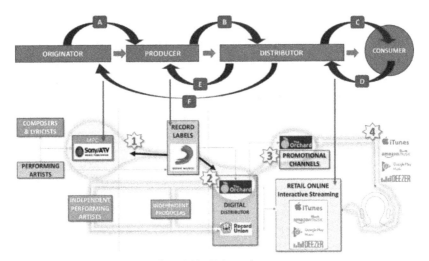

Figure 144 – Value exchange

**Symmetric competitors**

**Originator car**

The members of the originator car can be organized into three groups: the composers and lyricists, who receive the musical composition copyrights; the performing artists, who receive the sound recording copyrights; and the Music Publishing Companies (MPC), which offer a service of managing the musical composition copyrights to composers and lyricists.

I decided not to include composers, lyricists and performing artists in this competition analysis as they are not companies.

However, the MPCs, such as Sony/ATV, symmetrically compete with each other. The major competitors are: Sony/ATV Music Publishing, Universal Music Publishing Group, Warner/Chappell Music, BMG, Kobalt Music Group, Round Hill Music, SONGS Music Publishing, Black River Entertainment and Words & Music.

**Producer**

The symmetric competition occurs within the record labels. The biggest competitors are Sony Music Entertainment (Sony Music), Universal Music Publishing Group, Warner Music Group (including Warner Bros. Records and Atlantic Records), Island Records (a division of the Universal Music Group), BMG Rights Management, ABC-Paramount Records, Virgin Records, Red Hill Records, Atlantic Records and Def Jam Recordings.

**Distributors**

There are five different groups coexisting in the distributor train:

    1) the traditional promotional channel members

    2) the traditional sales structure members

    3) the digital distribution members

4) non-interactive streaming online retail

5) interactive streaming online retail

Symmetric competition occurs within the members of groups 2, 4 and 5.

- Symmetric competitors in the traditional sales structure members: retail chains vs. independent stores

- Symmetric competitors in non-interactive streaming online retail: Pandora, SiriusXM, AM/FM broadcasting stations

- Symmetric competitors in interactive streaming online retail: Spotify, Apple Music, Google Play, iTunes

From the perspective of this case, focusing on SONY and iTunes, the only symmetric competition identified occurs within the players that offer interactive streaming service.

**Asymmetric competitors**

**Originators**: I could not identify asymmetric competitors in this car, as there is only one group of companies (MPC).

**Producers**: I could not identify asymmetric competitors in this car, as there is only one group of companies (Record Label).

**Distributors:** Again, let´s consider the five different groups coexisting in the distributor train:

1) the traditional promotional channel members;

2) the traditional sales structure members;

3) the digital distribution members;

4) non-interactive streaming online retail;

5) interactive streaming online retail

Asymmetric competition occurs between the members of groups 2, 4 and 5: the traditional sales structure members vs. non-interactive streaming online retail (Pandora, SiriusXM, AM/FM broadcasting stations) vs. interactive streaming online retail (Spotify, Apple Music, Google Play, iTunes). They all compete for the revenue from consumers.

Another asymmetric competition occurs between the members of groups 1 and 3: the traditional promotional channel members (radio, print, video, retail, public relations) vs. the digital distribution members (Youtube, Facebook and other social networks, internet radio, podcasts and blogs). They compete to offer marketing services to Record Labels and Digital Distributors.

**Competition between members**

It is possible to see some types of competition that are not restrained to one specific car. For example, record labels and music publishing companies asymmetrically compete for copyrights revenue. One example is the recent dispute between Music Publishing Association and Spotify after Spotify announced they would only pay sound recording copyrights (to Record Labels) and would stop paying music composition copyrights to composers and lyricists (through MPCs).

Another asymmetric competition between members of different cars involves the Record Labels, digital distributors and promotional channels. They all offer marketing services to performing artists.

# Media Industry Case Study

## 13. Media industry: data value templates

### The company and the selected business unit

The "Grupo Folha" (GF), an important media conglomerate founded in Brazil in 1921, controls the newspaper with the largest circulation (Folha de São Paulo, FSP), the main Internet service and content provider (UOL) in the country, the biggest Brazilian commercial printing facility and other business units:

| Companies / Business Units | Description |
|---|---|
| UOL | The leading Internet portal in Brazil |
| Valor Econômico | The leading Brazilian business daily newspaper |
| Plural | A joint-venture with US-based Quad/Graphics; is the largest offset printing operation in South America. |
| SPDL | A 50/50 joint-venture with the Estado Group, the company delivers newspapers for both partners. |
| Folha de São Paulo (FSP) | Newspaper |
| Agora | Newspaper |
| Alô Negócios | Newspaper |
| Magazine Division | Responsible for guides and magazines that are distributed as free inserts within FSP. |
| Datafolha | One of the leading polling organizations in Brazil |
| Folhapress | News agency |
| Publifolha | A publishing house for documents on journalism, tourism, languages, cooking and children's tales. |
| Três Estrelas | A premium imprint for documents on Humanities |
| Livraria Folha | Online document store |
| Transfolha | A delivery company that distributes print products and e-commerce packages |

| Folha Gráfica | Printing services for corporations, publishing houses and advertising agencies |
|---|---|

Figure 145 - FSP Group

The selected business is the operation of the newspaper Folha de São Paulo (FSP), which has had the highest number of readers for the last three decades. In 2012, when it started charging for the Internet content, 11% of consumers used online subscriptions – today nearly 50% of the 20 million readers pay for the online content. This business unit has five companies that produce content, print and distribute newspapers, control the payment process, manage data storage and provide distance learning and generate a US$ 1.3 billion revenue per year.

This business unit has been facing drops in circulation and loss of revenue from classified advertising. In 2016, for the first time, the number of subscribers of the digital version surpassed the subscribers of the printed version and achieved 51% of total consumers (vs. 4% in 2010).

| 2010 | 2011 | 2012 | 2013 | 2014 | 2015 | 2016 |
|---|---|---|---|---|---|---|
| 4 | 8 | 13 | 20 | 38 | 43 | 51 |

Figure 146 – Printed version consumers (%)

Although the number of digital-only subscriptions has increased, the figures illustrated in Image 2 basically results from the reduction of subscribers in the printed version. Additionally, FSP faces a dramatic reduction in the value and frequency of advertisements. An urgent turnaround strategy is required.

**Brainstorming**

Based on the scenario described in the previous part, three questions were postulated:

Q1. How to revert the churn rate and stop the reduction of subscribers in the printed version of the FSP newspaper?

Q2. How to stop the decrease in sales revenue, including subscribers and publicity?

Q3. How to increase sales revenue trend observed over the last many years?

As mentioned by Prof. David Rogers, sometimes we answer the strategic questions "with simple careful application of strategic thinking".

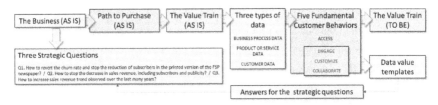

Figure 147 – Strategic thinking

**Path-to-Purchase**

The newspapers are produced and then transported to four distribution centers (DCs) where they are prepared for transportation to the consumers. The existing data management neglects the consumer user experience from 6:30am to 11:00pm. As long as FSP does not capture the data associated to the consumer experience cycle, they will not understand the entire path-to-purchase and no strategy will be able to create the differentiated value. There is an opportunity associated to understanding the user behavior.

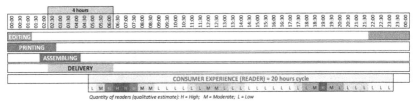

Figure 148 – Experience cycle

218

## The Value Train Analysis (simplified)

The FSP operation controls the entire value chain as the reporters, photographers and other employees are in the originator train, the editors and the printing facility in the producer train and a logistics operator responsible for newspaper distribution to final consumers occupies the distributor train.

The content is produced by reporters and photographers. The layouts of the page are prepared by the editors (A) and then the material follows for printing. Then, (B) the newspapers are sent to the distribution centers and (C) delivered to consumers. The (D) consumers pay for the newspaper.

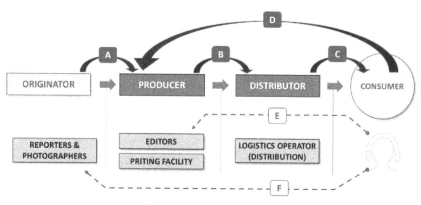

Figure 149 – Value train analysis

The basis of this data strategy is to capture consumer behavior data and make it available to (E) the editors and to (F) the reporters and originators. This will provide new relevant information to improve the quality of the product and to orientate reporters, photographers and publishers on how to do that.

## Capturing and using strategic data

The technology used to capture consumer behavior data will be QR codes. In this specific case, the QR code will generate strategic data capable to initiate a business turnaround and boost new revenue streams.

The idea is to associate a QR code to articles in each section and encourage the readers to "read" the codes with their smartphones and interact to produce data (see Figure 150).

Figure 150 – QR Code – example

The QR codes will capture consumer behavior and stimulate collaboration to enhance the quality of the product.

| Data Type & Utility | |
| --- | --- |
| A. Product or service data | |
| Deliver the core value proposition of the business product or service | A1. Reporters & Photographers |
| | A2. Comments & Reviews |
| | A3. Theme & sections |
| | A4. Figures, graphs, pictures |
| | A5. Long vs. short |
| B. Customer data | |
| Provide a complete picture of the customer and allow for more relevant and valuable interactions | B1. Reward vs links |
| | B2. Quantity vs daytime |
| | B3. Time in the day |
| | B4. Reading channels |
| | B5. Age, Gender, Profession |
| | B6. Location |
| | B7. Days of the week |
| | B8. Charge publicity |
| | B9. Total time |

Figure 151 – Type of data and utility

**Using the Data Value Templates (see slide 16)**

The use of QR codes combined to an APP, enables the interaction with subscribers and non-subscribers (limited number of interactions). The direct impact of data gathering will enable a solid strategy with the value templates.

The variety of data will reveal the yet unseen consumer behavior and allow FSP to determine various correlations (not necessarily causations). This initial process is associated (A1) to the INSIGHT template.

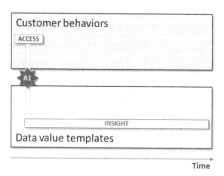

Figure 152 – Value template - Insight

**Insight Template**

By focusing on the ACCESS behavior, the media group FSP addresses the existing gap in the Path to Purchase and begins to perceive the customer experience behavior. It also solves the need to connect consumer-based data to the editors´ activity (see Figure 148, red line E).

The customized content will reduce the churn rate as word-of-mouth promotes access; this will enable the number of subscriptions to increase, differently from what has happened in recent years.

221

As the QR codes provide a variety of options to interact with the consumer, it generates product or service-related data. People of different ages, genders or from different locations, will have specific preferences. This could promote certain types of photos, for example – preferring either people or landscapes on the images. This information will enhance the quality of user experience when guidelines are adopted for specific sections of the newspaper.

**Personalization Template**

The more accessible the solution is, the more network interactions will occur. The capacity to tailor the content increases as a second consumer behavior becomes more intense: collaboration. For example, readers' comments enable the publisher to improve content relevance based on preferences for themes or sections, quality, format or content of figures, graphs and pictures and the length of the news. This product-related information enables corporate orientation on how or what to include in each edition. Therefore, reporters, photographers, editors and all staff will be able to dedicate efforts in a customer-driven environment.

Although the PERSONALIZATION template becomes important even before the consumer collaboration consolidates, it is only with this collaborative behavior that the quality of the product will increase (A2).

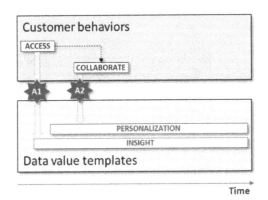

Figure 153 – Value template - Personalization

At this point, it is expected that the churn rate has reduced as another strategic association occurs between consumers' collaborative behavior and the personalization template. A customer's different affinities and interests can be identified, which is only possible by the continuous influx of insights (first template).

As FSP offers access and collaboration, the consumers will respond with engagement and more personal information including social data, and the use of pools may be requested to improve targeting (A3).

Targeting, together with insights and personalization, enable the identification of clusters of consumers. This visibility is important to create relevance to advertisers. For example, the publisher may generate a survey on the banking sector brand equity to have better arguments to negotiate specific publicity fees with the banks. As a consequence of this comprehensive process, the FSP provides a customized ecosystem to their readers (A4).

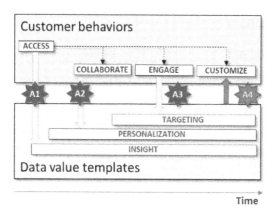

Figure 154 – Value template - Ecosystem

**Future benefits and metrics**

**Revert churn rate**

To inhibit the churn rate, the first step is to create a mechanism to access customers' data and understand their behaviors. I described that the use of QR codes via APP facilitates a massive access for readers to the platform, even those who are not yet subscribers.

Therefore, the management of this data fills a gap in the Path to Purchase cycle, which allows FSP to work on the domain of the INSIGHT value template.

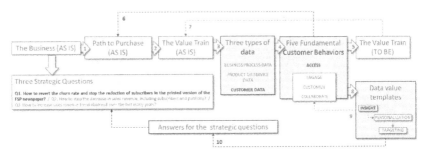

Figure 155 – Strategic thinking (b)

At this moment, three types of metrics can be used to measure scale, active usage and engagement. [see this video]

To measure scale, FSP can monitor the number of unique visitors, total number of visitors, month-on-month (MOM) growth in registrations, total number of interactions with the QR codes and number of downloads of the App.

To measure the active use, it is possible to control the number of daily active users (DAU), the total number of active users, the ratio of new users to repeat users/customers, the conversion rate (non-subscribers that interact who become subscribers), and churn rate.

Finally, as engagement indicators, FSP can estimate the reading time per users, customer satisfaction index, number of downloads, sources of traffic sources, posts contributed, number of likes and shares. At that point, the calculation of ROI (return on investment) should also be implemented.

## Revert existing sales reduction pattern

The access and engagement behaviors enable FSP to enter the domain of the personalization value template. Controlling information about their consumers can develop specific Path to Purchase cycles and advertisers.

By addressing specific actions to clusters of consumers, FSP adds value to its product strongly enough to sustain existing fees to new subscribers and future advertisers. Having a better knowledge of their consumers, FSP can attract companies that currently advertise in other types of media.

As illustrated in Image 155 (see information in blue), the existing combination of customer behaviors (access and engagement) and the dynamics in the data value templates (insight and personalization) enables FSP to connect to end users and changes the Value Train landscape.

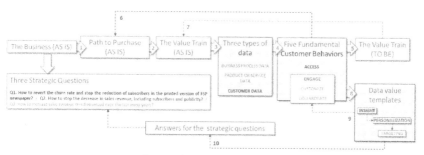

Figure 156 – Strategic thinking (c)

As engagement indicators 2, FSP can use the following:

- Estimation of the reading time per users
- Customer satisfaction index
- Number of downloads
- Traffic sources
- Posts contributed
- Number of likes and shares
- Sales (frequency and value) from subscribers and announcers.

225

At that point, the calculation of ROI (return on investment) must be closely monitored as a significant pattern change is expected.

**Increase sales revenue**

The strategic movements explained address the questions related to (a) reducing the churn rate and (b) sustaining the business in the existing level of interactions and revenue.

Basically, not to get worse and keep it like it is today. Considering the FSP subscriber numbers have decreased over the last 20 years and the frequency of advertisements and the value paid for each announcement have both dramatically decreased in recent years, these two promised benefits represent a sound turnaround in the organization. However, that is not enough.

Over time, consumers tend to engage more complementary behavior such as collaboration (see Figure 156, in green) will be part of the business ecosystem – this behavior and its interaction with the targeting domain.

The continuous data sharing, expanding to social information, will enable FSP to produce commercial proposals to industry sectors that have never heavily announced in the newspaper, such as fast food, insurance, healthcare, combining print and online versions on different scales – from massive announcements in multiple channels and newspaper sectors, to micro announcements associated to specific news.

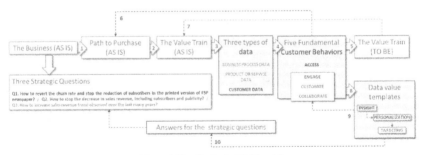

Figure 157 – Strategic thinking (d)

This approach enhances consumer behavior associated to customizations and creates new revenue sources for the business. This third phase completes the digital maturity roadmap to be followed according to a strategically thought schedule with clear milestones and ownership (the definition of this schedule is not addressed in this case).

The measures of this phase should focus on the revenue generation from new subscribers, new publicity channels, new publicity formats and new advertisers. It is important to understand that these are the benefits to be achieved after a long process that requires internal cultural adaptation and the understanding of commercial practices in sectors that are not traditionally in the newspaper ecosystem.

Another important change is in the average value for the publicity ticket – it is likely that the sales landscape moves from a few large advertisers to many smaller announcers. This will require an adaptation of personnel and organizational structure.

# List of Experts

Link to the expert´s cited in the book (LINDEDIN Profile)

------------------------------------------------------------------------

**Remember to** Personalize Your Connection Requests (by Tammy Borden)

> *"don't simply click the "connect" button. If you do, a generic request will be sent. Instead, go to the person's profile page and click the "connect" button there. Doing so will bring up the box shown below and allow you to add a personal note with your connection request..."*

**You may copy/paste the following message:**

"Dear nonono
I've read one of your articles that is cited in the book "Business Strategies for Digital Transformation" (Alexandre Oliveira) and would like to connect.
Best, nonono"

------------------------------------------------------------------------

1. Abdul Al Lily
2. Abhinav Rai
3. Adam Farmer
4. Adam Singer
5. Ahmad Asadullah
6. Albena Pergelova
7. Aleks Buczkowski
8. Alexander K. Fleisher
9. Alexandre Oliveira
10. Andreas Weiss
11. Andrei Hagiu
12. Andrew Zangre
13. Anisha Garg
14. Ankit Prakash
15. Anne Rozinat
16. Anniina Heinikangas
17. Atreyi Kankanhalli
18. B. Edelman
19. Bala Iyer
20. Benjamin Edelman
21. Carol Esmark Jones
22. Christian Barney
23. Christine Whittemore
24. Christopher Koch
25. Christopher Koch
26. Chuck Schaeffer
27. Clint Boulton
28. Clodagh O'Brien
29. Craig Smith
30. Dan Vesset
31. Darren W. Dahl
32. David Armano
33. David Fumo
34. David Rogers
35. David S. Evans
36. David Sutcliffe
37. DeSarbo,Wayne S.
38. Dorothée Laire
39. Ed Ku and Yi Wen Fan
40. Elizabeth J. Altman
41. Enric Durany
42. Evan Tan
43. Fernando Angulo
44. Fred Donovan
45. Gary Mortimer
46. Gary Thome
47. Gaurav Bhalla
48. Geoffrey G. Parker

49. George Corbin
50. Greg Finn
51. Greg Satell
52. Grzegorz Piechota
53. H.O. Maycotte
54. Heather Mcdonald
55. Hector Bonilla
56. Hilton Barbour
57. Hitesh Bhasin
58. Holly Chessman
59. Howard Tiersky
60. Isam Faik
61. Ivana Taylor
62. Jacinda Santora
63. Jacqueline De Gernier
64. James Chen
65. James Currier
66. James Lovejoy
67. Jean-Pierre Calabretto
68. Jeff Berman
69. Jeff Korhan
70. *Jeff Weinstein*
71. Jennifer Lund
72. Jerry (Yoram) Wind
73. Jerry Wind
74. Joe Pinsker
75. John Spacey
76. Jonah Berger
77. Josep Rialp
78. Joseph Michael
79. Jukka P. Saarinen
80. Juri Mattila
81. Justin M. Jacobson
82. Kathryn Gessner
83. Katrina Wakefield
84. Kelsey Butterworth

85. Kunal Patel
86. Larry Alton
87. Larry Myler
88. Len Markidan
89. Lindsay Kolowich
90. Louis Columbus
91. Louise Grimmer
92. Lynda M. Belcher
93. Madeline Bennett
94. Mark Bonchek
95. Marshall W. Alstyne
96. Martha Heller
97. Martin Kirov
98. Megan Dickey
99. Melissa Lafsky
100. Michael J. Garbade
101. Michael L. Tushman
102. Michael Shostak
103. Michael Sorich
104. Mika Raunio
105. Mike Friedrichsen
106. Nadja Nordling
107. Nandita Bose
108. Naren Chawla
109. Nicholas Shields
110. Nick Hoffman
111. Nick Ismail
112. Nico van Eijk
113. Nicolai van Gorp
114. Nicolas Bry
115. Orla Lynskey
116. Pam Moore
117. Peep Laja
118. Peter B. Nichol
119. Peter Murray
120. Peter Weill

121. Pier Luca Lanzi
122. Pieter Nooren
123. Raj Ramesh
124. Rajdeep Grewal
125. Rajesh V. Manchanda
126. Richard Malone
127. Rina Henderson
128. Ronan O Fathaigh
129. Ross Jeffery
130. Ryan Baumann
131. Salvatore Parise
132. Sangeet Choudary
133. Sara Toole
134. Sarwant Singh
135. Shafqat Islam
136. Shivam Arora
137. Sophia Tran
138. Stephanie Woerner
139. Steve Banker
140. Sukesh Mudrakola
141. Sung Lee, Liming Zhu
142. Suzanne Trevellyan
143. Taina Ketola
144. Tammy Borden
145. Terrie Nolinske
146. Timo Seppälä
147. Tom Davenport
148. Tomas Kellner
149. Vanhishikha Bhargava
150. Will Kenton
151. Yahya Kamalipour
152. Yuri Shub
153. Zaw Thiha Tun

# Remissive Index